RUDOLF STEINER (1861–1925) called his spiritual philosophy 'anthroposophy', meaning 'wisdom of the human being'. As a highly developed seer, he based his work on direct knowledge and perception of spiritual dimensions. He initiated a modern and universal 'science of spirit', accessible to anyone willing to exercise clear and unprejudiced thinking.

From his spiritual investigations Steiner provided suggestions for the renewal of many activities, including education (both general and special), agriculture, medicine, economics, architecture, science, philosophy, religion and the arts. Today there are thousands of schools, clinics, farms and other organizations involved in practical work based on his principles. His many published works feature his research into the spiritual nature of the human being, the evolution of the world and humanity, and methods of personal development. Steiner wrote some 30 books and delivered over 6000 lectures across Europe. In 1924 he founded the General Anthroposophical Society, which today has branches throughout the world.

THE MYSTERIES OF THE HOLY GRAIL

From Arthur and Parzival to Modern Initiation

RUDOLF STEINER

Compiled and edited by Matthew Barton

RUDOLF STEINER PRESS

For Sibylle and Henk

Rudolf Steiner Press
Hillside House, The Square
Forest Row, RH18 5ES

www.rudolfsteinerpress.com

Published by Rudolf Steiner Press 2010

For earlier English publications, see Sources section on p. 215

Originally published in German in various volumes of the GA (*Rudolf Steiner Gesamtausgabe* or Collected Works) by Rudolf Steiner Verlag, Dornach. For further information see Sources, p. 215. This authorized translation is published by permission of the Rudolf Steiner Nachlassverwaltung, Dornach

All material has been translated or checked against the original German by Matthew Barton

A catalogue record for this book is available from the British Library

ISBN: 978 1 85584 234 2

Cover by Andrew Morgan Design
Typeset by DP Photosetting, Neath, West Glamorgan
Printed and bound by Cromwell Press Group,
Trowbridge, Wiltshire

Contents

V. THE WAR-TORN SOUL AND THE QUEST FOR INTEGRATION

VI. THE GRAIL IN THE HUMAN ORGANISM: SPIRIT INFUSING MATTER

VII. INITIATION TODAY: THE TRIALS AND THE QUEST

Introduction

There is a good deal of debate and disagreement about the etymology of the name 'Parzival', and still more about the origins of the word 'Grail'. These are discussions, however, which I don't wish to delve too deeply into here, as they seem somewhat secondary to the saga itself and the multiple meanings we ourselves can invest it with. The symbolism and significance of a legend or a story ultimately depends on how we ourselves absorb it: how it connects with strata of the psyche we bear within us that, as it were, await the tug of the tale to come to our full awareness. A story that really speaks to the human soul will inevitably have a depth and complexity that lures the rational mind to the threshold of mysteries it only dimly grasps, rather as we wrestle with the 'meaning' of a dream. A true story (and clearly I don't mean 'factual') speaks to our deepest impulses because it was originally born from them. The Parzival saga is a true story in this sense, concealing in its meandering progressions and vivid tableaux a multiplicity of meanings that intellectual interpretations alone cannot begin to fathom.

In one sense the story is authentic because the quest and exploits of its heroes strangely mirror many of our own, often thwarted efforts at understanding it. We have to go deeper, learn more about ourselves, if it is really to speak to us, just as Parzival suffers setbacks in his long quest for self-knowledge. The diversity and complexity of Rudolf Steiner's own quest to understand this saga are a tribute both to its many possible meanings and to his willingness to 'entertain' them without easy simplification; to look for the multifaceted truth from many different yet complementary angles. Though the saga dates from around the twelfth century, Steiner finds extraordinary modern and future relevance in it. Like seeking to approach the Grail itself, you get a sense that you cannot force the legend to disclose itself but that its meanings, instead, will increasingly dawn on you as you become more worthy of it.

So I will refrain from further analyses here and invite you instead to saddle the steed of your willing attention and set off into this legend, and Steiner's thoughts about it, with all the perspicacity you can muster. The name 'Parzival' itself[1]—whether these etymologies are suspect or not—has been interpreted as meaning, among other things, either 'Pierce-the-valley' (*percer le val*) or 'Pierce-the-veil' (*percer le voile*). Certainly Parzival must encounter and engage with the veils of illusion, and valleys of shadow and doubt, as we must too. The resonance of his name with 'perceive', though this etymology is very likely spurious, also strikes me as significant. We perceive most truly, after all, when we persevere, probe and pierce through to levels of vision beyond merely given sight.

If possible, if you do not already know the saga, I recommend reading a version of it—either the epic by Wolfram von Eschenbach or a summary of it—before embarking on this journey. For those who do not have the time or patience for this, the penultimate section of this volume does, very briefly, recount some of the most important episodes, interspersed with passages by Steiner; and it would be possible to start this book from the 'wrong end' if you wish, then return to the beginning with a little more sense of the story's trajectory.

As to the much-disputed and elusive meaning and etymology of the word 'Grail'—almost as elusive, interestingly, as the thing itself, if indeed it is a 'thing' at all—the only thought I offer here is this: the word is very possibly derived, at least partly, both from the medieval Latin noun *gradail* or *gradale* meaning a vase, goblet or basin, and from the older Latin word *gradalis* or also *gradualis*, which is connected with 'gradually'. How a vessel and a slow progression can be linked might not immediately be apparent, except perhaps if one thinks of a ritual procession such as Parzival witnesses at the Grail castle. But still more helpful, to me at least, is a sense that the vessel of the Grail only very gradually descends towards us and comes into focus as we raise ourselves individually to it by piercing through the illusions of materialism, acknowledging that we ourselves can ultimately become true vessels for the spirit.

If we assume for a moment that the Grail is a state towards which we are evolving, which we therefore cannot yet fully know but which we carry within us as a seed of growing potential, it cannot then be a single fixed object or meaning; and certainly not an increasingly distant bloodline 'relating' solely to some past and merely physically-determined glory. In this sense Steiner's approach is powerfully invigorating and revitalizing, for he makes clear that Christ can only be with us 'to the end of the world' as a force that carries us beyond ties of blood and narrow, racial communities to an ever more unifying and luminous humanity. But such harmony cannot of course be imposed—it must rise out of each of us, like a new language, as we grow slowly and laboriously in love and understanding. Just as the three key protagonists of the Parzival legend—Parzival himself, Gawain and Feirefiz—fight each other before recognizing that the 'other' is in fact their 'brother', so we must struggle and wrestle our way through to a wholly earned, compassionate fraternity by way of full assertion and realization of our individual qualities. There is of course still a very long way to go, but the Grail legend accompanies us on that journey.

Matthew Barton

I

THE GOSPEL OF JOHN AND THE VIRGIN SOPHIA

1. Christian Catharsis: the Purified Soul

Extract from a lecture given in Hamburg on 18 May 1908

The suggestion below that we should be 'fertilized by what streams into us from the world of spirit' rather than focusing exclusively on our own inner processes, is a fitting prelude to the Grail theme. We can cleanse or purify ourselves so that we open to the influx of powers in the cosmos, developing and enhancing our nature through them. The related theme of sexuality as 'given' human experience that can be raised to a conscious spiritual sphere, and ultimately transformed, is also one that will recur throughout this book. Here we find the purified, receptive human soul embodied in the figure of the mother of Jesus (known as the 'Virgin Sophia' in the esoteric tradition), and can thus make an immediate and direct connection with the life and deed of Christ, which is essential for understanding the Grail and our human response to it. The Gospel of St John also clearly has an intimate connection with the originating Word or Logos, and we will later see how Steiner connects the Grail quest with the life-creating potential inherent in human utterance.

We must understand that when a person has attained this [Rosicrucian] initiation he is fundamentally quite different from the person he was before it. While formerly he was only associated with the things of the physical world, he now acquires the possibility likewise of associating with events and beings of the world of spirit. This presupposes that we acquire knowledge in a much more real way than in that abstract, dry, prosaic sense in which we usually refer to knowledge. A person who acquires spiritual knowledge finds the process to be something quite different—a complete realization of that beautiful expression 'Know thyself'. The most dangerous thing in the realm of knowledge, however, is to misunderstand these words; and nowadays this occurs all too frequently. Many construe them to mean that they should no longer look about the physical world but should gaze into their own inner being and seek there for everything spiritual. This is a very mistaken understanding of the saying, for that is not at all what it means. We must clearly understand that true higher knowledge is also an evolution from one standpoint which the human being has attained to another he had not previously reached. If we practise self-knowledge only by brooding on ourselves, we see only what we already possess. We acquire nothing new by this process, but only knowledge of our own lower self in the present meaning of that word. This inner nature is only one aspect necessary for knowledge, and must be complemented by the other aspect. Without both there is no real knowledge. Through our inner nature we can develop organs by which we gain knowledge. But just as the eye, as an external sense organ, would not perceive the sun by gazing into itself, but only by looking outwards to the sun, so the inner perceptive organs must gaze outwards, or in other words into an external spiritual realm in order to actually perceive. The concept of 'knowledge' had a much deeper, more real meaning in former ages. When we read in the Bible that Abraham or some other patriarch 'knew his wife' we soon find that this means fertilization and reproduction. If you consider the words 'Know thyself' in Greek, they do not mean that you should stare into your own inner being but that you should be fertilized by what streams into you from the world of spirit. [. . .]

Two things are necessary for this to happen: firstly a self-preparation through catharsis and illumination, and secondly an opening of our inner being freely to the world of spirit. Here we may liken our inner nature to the female aspect, and the outer content of the spiritual world to the male. The inner being must be made sensitive and receptive to the higher self. When this happens, the higher human self streams into us from the world of spirit. We can ask where this higher human self is. Is it somewhere within us as individuals? No, it is not. On Saturn, Sun and Moon,[2] the higher self was diffused over the entire cosmos. At that time the cosmic I was spread out across all humankind; but now we have to permit it to work upon us, upon our previously prepared inner nature. This means that our inner human nature—the astral body—must be cleansed, purified and ennobled and must undergo catharsis. Then the spirit can stream into us from without, illuminating us. This will happen when our astral body has undergone a catharsis that develops inner organs of perception. [. . .]

This cleansed, purified astral body which, at the moment of illumination, bears within it none of the impure impressions of the physical world but only the organs of perception of the spiritual world, is called the 'pure, chaste, wise virgin Sophia' in esoteric Christianity. Through all we receive as pupils in catharsis, we cleanse and purify the astral body so that it transforms into the virgin Sophia. And when the virgin Sophia meets the cosmic I, the universal I which causes illumination, the pupil is surrounded by light, by spiritual light. In esoteric Christianity this second power that approaches the virgin Sophia is called the 'Holy Spirit'. In line with esoteric Christianity, therefore, it is true to say that through his processes of initiation the Christian esotericist purifies and cleanses his astral body; he makes his astral body into the virgin Sophia and is illumined from above—one might call it 'overshadowed'—by the Holy Spirit, the cosmic, universal I. Someone thus illumined—who in other words, in terms of esoteric Christianity, has received the 'Holy Spirit' into himself—speaks in a different way from then on. How does he speak? When he speaks of Saturn, Sun and Moon evolutionary stages, or the different aspects of the human being, or the processes of cosmic evolution, he is not expressing *his own* opinion. *His* views do not come into consideration at all. When such a person speaks about Saturn, it is Saturn itself that speaks through him. When he speaks of the sun, the spiritual being of the sun speaks through him. He is the instrument. His personal ego has been eclipsed—which means that at such moments it has become impersonal and the cosmic, universal I is using his ego as its instrument to speak through. [...]

Thus we have acquired two concepts, and found their spiritual significance. We have learned to know the nature of the virgin Sophia, which is the purified astral body, and the nature of the 'Holy Spirit', the cosmic universal I, which the virgin Sophia receives and which can then speak out of this purified astral body. There is something still more to be attained—a still higher stage: the ability to help someone else, to give him the impetus to accomplish both of these. At our stage of evolution people can receive the virgin Sophia (the purified astral body) and the Holy Spirit (illumination) in the manner described, but only Christ Jesus could give to the earth what was necessary to accomplish this. He has implanted in the spiritual part of the earth the forces which make it possible for this to happen at all. [...]

The events in Palestine not only have to do with the highly

evolved individuality of Jesus of Nazareth, who had passed through many incarnations and developed so highly that he needed such an extraordinary mother as the virgin Sophia, but also with a second mystery. When Jesus of Nazareth was 30 years old, what he had so far experienced enabled him to perform an exceptional action. We know that the human being consists of physical, etheric and astral bodies and I.[3] This fourfold human being is the earthly human being we know. But at a certain stage of evolution, at a particular moment, a person can withdraw his I or ego from the three bodies and abandon them, leaving them intact and entirely uninjured. This I then enters the worlds of spirit and the three bodies remain behind [. . .] and because the three bodies are so highly developed by the I that lived in them, they are fit instruments for a still higher being who now takes possession of them. In the thirtieth year of Jesus of Nazareth's life, the being we call Christ took possession of his physical, etheric and astral bodies. [. . .]

The corporeality of Jesus of Nazareth, from which he withdrew, was so mature and perfect that the sun Logos, the being of the six Elohim, which we have described as the being of the sun, was able to penetrate it. It could incarnate for three years in this corporeality, could become flesh. The sun Logos who can shine into human beings through illumination, the sun Logos Himself, the Holy Spirit, entered. The universal I, the cosmic I entered; and from then on, for three years, the sun Logos spoke through the body of Jesus. Christ speaks through the body of Jesus during these three years. This event is indicated in the Gospel of St John and also in the other Gospels as the descent of the dove, of the Holy Spirit, upon Jesus of Nazareth. At that moment, esoteric Christianity tells us that the I of Jesus of Nazareth left his body, and that from then on the Christ is in him, speaking, teaching and working through him. This is the first event that happens, according to the Gospel of St John. We now have the Christ within the astral, etheric and physical bodies of Jesus of Nazareth. There he worked as has been described, until the Mystery of Golgotha took place. What occurred at Golgotha? Let us consider that important moment when the blood flowed from the wounds of the crucified saviour. To help you understand this I will compare it with something else.

Let us suppose we have here a vessel filled with water. In the water salt is dissolved and the water becomes quite transparent. Because we have warmed the water we have made a salt solution. Now let us cool the water. The salt precipitates and we see how it condenses below and forms a deposit at the bottom of the vessel. That is the process for someone who sees only with physical eyes. For a person who sees with spiritual eyes, something else is happening. While the salt is condensing below, the spirit of the salt streams up through the water, permeating it. The salt can only become condensed when the spirit of the salt has departed from it and become diffused into the water. Those who understand these things know that wherever condensation takes place a spiritualization also always occurs. What thus condenses below has its counterpart above in the spiritual, just as, in the case of salt, the salt spirit streams upwards and disseminates when the salt condenses and is precipitated below. Thus it was not only a physical process that took place when the blood flowed from the wounds of the saviour, but it was actually accompanied by a spiritual process: that is, the Holy Spirit which was received at the Jordan baptism united with the earth; the Christ Himself flowed into the very being of the earth. From now on the earth was changed, and this is why, in earlier lectures, I told you that a person viewing the earth from a distant star would have observed its whole appearance altered by the Mystery of Golgotha. The sun Logos became a part of the earth, formed an alliance with it and became the spirit of the earth. He achieved this by entering the body of Jesus of Nazareth in his thirtieth year and remaining active there for three years, after which He continued to be embodied in the earth.

Now the important thing here is that this event must exert an effect on the true Christian; that it must give him something whereby he may gradually develop the beginnings of a purified astral body in the Christian sense. There had to be a power available to the Christian whereby he could make his astral body more and more like a virgin Sophia, and through it receive the Holy Spirit which was able to spread out over the entire earth, but which could not be received by anyone whose astral body did not resemble the virgin Sophia. What is this power? It consists in the fact of Christ Jesus entrusting to the 'disciple whom he loved'—the writer of the Gospel of St John—the mission of describing truly and faithfully, through his own illumination, the events in Palestine so that they might work upon human beings. If people allow what is written in the Gospel of St John to work sufficiently on them, their astral body will embark on the process of becoming a virgin Sophia, will become receptive to the Holy Spirit. Gradually, through the strength of this impulse emanating from the Gospel, it will first feel and perceive the true spirit. Jesus Christ entrusted this mission to the writer of the Gospel. You need only read it: The mother of Jesus—the virgin Sophia in esoteric Christianity—stands at the foot of the cross; and from the cross Christ says to the disciple whom He loved: '"Henceforth this is thy mother." And from this hour the disciple took her unto himself.' This means: The force which was in my astral body and made it capable of bearing the Holy Spirit, I now give to you; write down what this astral body has been able to acquire through its development. 'And the disciple took her unto himself' means that he wrote the Gospel of St John. And in this Gospel the writer concealed forces which develop the virgin Sophia. At the cross he was entrusted with the mission of receiving these forces as his mother and of being the true, authentic interpreter of the Messiah. This really means that if you live wholly in accordance with the Gospel of St John and understand it spiritually, it has the power to lead you to Christian catharsis, to give you the virgin Sophia. Then the Holy Spirit, united with the earth, will grant you illumination or what early Christianity calls *photismos*. And what the most intimate disciples experienced in Palestine was so powerful that from then on they possessed the capacity to perceive in the world of spirit. The most intimate disciples received this capacity. Perceiving in the spirit, in the Christian sense, means that we transform our astral body to such a degree through the power of the events in Palestine that what we see need not be before us in an external, physical and sensory way. [...] If we try to make into a feeling, into experience, what we can learn from spiritual science about the Gospel of St John, we shall then find that this Gospel is not a textbook but a force that can be active within our souls. [...]

2. The Birth of Higher Perception

Extract from a lecture given in Kassel on St John's day 1909

Building further on the Gospel of St John, Steiner here identifies the Grail as the essence of potential higher life within us, which is rooted in the revitalizing deed of Christ. The image of the Rose Cross—the black wood from which red roses spring—is one of death in matter as a precondition for rejuvenation through the spirit, and here appears intimately connected with the Grail theme.

When we behold, in the world around us, the various things which our eyes perceive and our hands touch, we observe how they arise and decay. We see how the flowers blossom and wither, and how the year's whole vegetation comes to life and dies away; and though there are things in the world such as mountains and rocks, apparently defying the ages, the proverb 'continual drops of water wear a stone' points to a premonition in the human soul that the very rocks and mountains, in all their majesty, are subject to the laws of the temporal world. We know that whatever is formed from the elements grows and decays; and this applies not only to our bodily form but also to the temporal self. Those who know how a spiritual world may be attained, however, are aware that though our eyes, ears, and other senses do not help with this, we may nevertheless enter the world of spirit through awakening, rebirth, initiation. And what is reborn?

When we look within ourselves, we can ultimately discover that within the inner self is the being we refer to as 'I'. The 'I' is distinguished, by virtue of its very name, from all things of the exterior world. To every exterior thing a name may be applied from without. We can all call the table 'table', and the clock 'clock'. The word 'I', however, can never fall upon our ears from without if we ourselves are meant, for this word ('I') must be uttered from within. To every other being we are 'you'. This fact in itself enables us to distinguish between this ego being and all else within and around ourselves. But to this we must add something which spiritual investigators of all ages have repeatedly emphasized for the benefit of mankind, through their own experience: that within this 'I' another, a higher ego, is born, as the child is born of the mother.

When we consider the human being as he passes through life, we see him first as a child, clumsy in respect of his surroundings, and merely beholding things. Gradually and by degrees he learns to understand these things; we see how his intelligence awakens, how his will and intellect grow, and how he increases in strength and energy. But individuals can advance in another way too, developing further, beyond mundane realities; they can reach the point, so to speak, of finding a second I which, looking down upon the first, can say 'you' to it, even as the ordinary I says 'you' to the external world and to its own body.

Thus a distant ideal of the human soul can become actuality for those who follow guidance from the spiritual investigator and say to themselves: 'The self I have known hitherto is involved in the outer world and passes away with it. But a second self slumbers in me—a self of which people are often unaware, though it is as much united with the eternal as the first self is united with the transitory and the temporal.'

When this rebirth occurs, the higher I can behold a world of spirit in the same way that the lower I can perceive the sensory world through the senses. This so-called awakening, rebirth, or initiation is the greatest event the human soul can experience, a view held also by those who called themselves Rosicrucians, whose emblem was the Rose Cross. They knew that this birth of the higher self—which can look down upon the lower self as someone looks upon the outer world—is intrinsically connected with the advent of Jesus Christ. That is to say: just as an individual human being can experience a new birth in the course of his life and development, a new birth for the whole of humanity took place through Christ Jesus. The individual experience of the birth of the higher I as an inner, mystic and spiritual event was enacted for the whole of humanity as a historical fact in the outer world through Christ Jesus in Palestine. [. . .]

The evangelists set themselves the task firstly of showing that Christ Jesus issues from the primal spirit of the world, indeed from God Himself. The divinity hitherto concealed in all mankind becomes pre-eminently manifest in Christ Jesus. This is the same God of whom it is said in the Gospel of St John that He was there in the beginning. And it was the aim of the evangelists to show that this God and no other was in Jesus of Nazareth. [. . .]

The Christians of St John, whose symbol was the Rose Cross, said that humanity's higher self, reborn through the Mystery of Golgotha, has been preserved intact. It was preserved by that exclusive community which developed within Rosicrucianism. This continuity is indicated symbolically in the legend of the sacred vessel called the 'Holy Grail', from which Christ Jesus ate and drank and in which the blood which flowed from His wounds was gathered by Joseph of Arimathea. This vessel, they say, was brought to Europe by angels. A temple was built for it and the Rosicrucians became the guardians of its content: that is, of what constitutes the very essence of the reborn God. The mystery of the reborn God continued to be cultivated—the mystery of the Holy Grail. It is presented to us as a new Gospel. The wise and revered author of the Gospel of St John could say:

> *In the beginning was the Word, and the Word was with God, and the Word was a God. The same that was in the beginning with God has been born again in Him whom we saw suffer and die upon Golgotha and who is risen again.*

The continuity of the divine principle through all ages and its resurrection is described by the writer of the Gospel of St John. But the narrators of such things knew that that which existed from the beginning is preserved unchanged:

> *In the beginning was the mystery of the higher human I; the same was preserved in the Grail, and remained united with it. In the Grail lives the I which is united with the eternal and the immortal, even as the lower I is united with the transitory and mortal.*

Whoever knows the mystery of the Holy Grail knows that from the wood of the cross springs living, budding life, the immortal self symbolized by the roses sprouting from the dark wood of the cross. Thus the mystery of the Rose Cross may be regarded as a continuation of the Gospel of St John and, in this respect, we may truly speak the following words:

> *In the beginning was the Word, and the Word was with God, and the Word was a God. The same was in the beginning with God. All things were made by Him and without Him was nothing made. In Him was life and the life was the light*

> *of men. And the light shone in the darkness and the darkness comprehended it not. Only a few, in whom something lived that was not born of the flesh, comprehended the light that shone in the darkness. Then the light became flesh and dwelt among men in the likeness of Jesus of Nazareth.*

And we can then continue:

> *And in Christ who dwelt in Jesus of Nazareth we see none other than the higher, divine self of all mankind, the God who came down to earth in Adam and was born again. This reborn human self was perpetuated as a sacred mystery; it was preserved in the symbol of the Rose Cross and is cultivated today as the mystery of the Holy Grail.*

The higher I which may be born in every human soul points to the rebirth of the divine I in the evolution of humanity through the events in Palestine. In the same way that the higher self can be born in every human being, the higher self of humanity as a whole was born in Palestine and is preserved and further developed behind the external symbol of the Rose Cross.

Thus we have the birth of the higher self in every individual human being, and a similar birth for humanity as a whole—the rebirth of the divine I. [. . .] A sharp distinction is needed here. We have a high initiate reborn as Jesus of Nazareth and, beyond this birth, something of significance in the spiritual world—something spiritual which will gradually develop the body until it becomes ripe for the spirit. When this point is reached, the event thus prepared is enacted. The Baptist approaches Jesus of Nazareth and a higher spirit descends upon him and unites with him; Christ enters the body of Jesus of Nazareth. John the Baptist, as the forerunner of Jesus of Nazareth, might well say: 'I came into the world and prepared the way for one mightier than I. I have preached that the kingdom of heaven is at hand and that people must change. I came among human beings and declared to them that a new impulse will enter mankind. As in spring the sun mounts higher in the heavens to proclaim the renewal of life, so I come to proclaim the new life which is the reborn self of humanity.'

When the human principle in Jesus of Nazareth had reached its highest development, and his body had become an expression of the spirit within him, he was ripe to receive the Christ in the baptism by John. His body had unfolded its full power, as the radiant sun on midsummer or St John's day. [. . .] The spirit was to be born out of the darkness, as the sun which increases in power and waxes strong till St John's day and then begins to wane. It was the Baptist's mission to proclaim this and to tell how the sun mounts on high with increasing splendour until the moment when he, the Baptist, could say: 'He who was announced by the prophets of old, the Son of the spiritual realms, born of the spirit, behold, He has appeared.' Up to this point John the Baptist was active. But, the way having once been prepared, when the days begin to shorten and the darkness again prevails, inner spirit light must shine forth ever more brightly, in the same way that Christ shines forth in Jesus of Nazareth.

John beheld the approach of Jesus of Nazareth, whose development he felt as his own increase, as the increase of the sun. 'I must henceforth decrease,' he said, 'as the sun decreases after Midsummer Day. But He, the spiritual sun, will increase and his light will shine forth out of the darkness.' [. . .]Thus was the universal I of humanity reborn, and the conditions fulfilled for the rebirth of the individual higher self in every human being.

II

FROM THE SPIRIT IN NATURE TO THE SPIRIT IN US: THE NEW INITIATION

3. From Arthur to Parzival

Extract from a lecture given in Torquay on 21 August 1924

Returning now to the origins of the Parzival saga, which has close connections with Arthurian legends yet represents an important departure from them, Steiner here highlights the nature of this distinction as the new 'earthing' of cosmic intelligence in human evolution. Arthurian Christianity looks out into the spirit in nature and the cosmos, whereas the Christianity of the Grail is one sought primarily within human beings. Just as Christ fully rooted spiritual worlds in earthly reality, so the Grail principle is that of an embodied and fully grounded spirit working through human hearts.

When conferring in council, King Arthur occupied the central seat with the 12 ranged in a circle round him; and over each hung a zodiac symbol, as emblem to show under which cosmic influence they stood. It was from this place that European civilization emanated. It was here that Arthur and his 12 absorbed from the sun the forces they needed to conduct their great campaigns throughout the rest of Europe, and to drive out from people the ancient demonic powers still widespread in the European population of the time. These 12 companions, led by King Arthur, battled to secure outer civilization.

If we ask ourselves how these 12 felt, what they felt themselves to be, we can only understand the nature of their fraternity if we return to what I just characterized. People did not feel intelligence to be dwelling inside them. They did not say: 'I work out my thoughts and intelligent ideas', but instead experienced intelligence as revelation, and sought such revelation through a group such as I described, a group of 12 or 13, together drawing in from without the intelligence they needed to form impetuses which would inform and affect civilization. And likewise they felt themselves as serving the power which we can call by the Christian and Hebrew name of Michael.[4] The whole configuration of King Arthur's castle shows that the group of 12 under King Arthur's leadership is a Michael community, from the time when Michael still dispensed cosmic intelligence.

Yes, this community is in fact what has held out longest to safeguard Michael's dominion over cosmic intelligence. And one can say that as we look out today over the ruins of Arthur's castle we can feel, preserved in the Akashic records, a sense of stones tumbling down still from what were once mighty castle gates; and as these stones fall down we can feel something like an earthly image of the lapse of intelligence, of cosmic intelligence, from the hands of Michael into the hearts and minds of human beings.

And alongside this Arthur–Michael stream, another, contrary stream arises at the place to which Christianity in more inward form had fled for refuge. This is the Grail stream, described in the legend of Parzival. In this Grail stream, too, we find 12 surrounding one figure, but now in a way that specifically takes account of the fact that intelligence, thoughts of an intelligent kind, no longer flow down from heaven to earth, but that what now flows down conducts itself in relation to earthly thoughts like the holy fool Parzival. This is what now flows down from the heavens, and intelligence is now only regarded as arising in the earthly domain.

Over here, in the north, stands Arthur's castle, where

people keep the flame of cosmic intelligence alive, and desire to integrate the intelligence of the universe with earthly civilization. And on the other hand there stands, as contrast to it, the Grail castle where intelligence is no longer invoked from the heavens but where the realization has dawned that human wisdom and heavenly wisdom are worlds apart. From this other castle in the south there streams out what can pour into the intelligence that has lapsed from the heavens.

And so, if we really penetrate what was happening here we can see in these ancient times—which also reach right into the period when the Mystery of Golgotha occurs over in Asia—the most fervent efforts undertaken by the Arthur principle on the one hand to safeguard Michael's cosmic dominion over intelligence, and on the other, starting in Spain, the Grail principle with its efforts to locate intelligence on earth in future, so that it does not need to stream down from the heavens. The whole Grail legend draws its breath from the sense of what I have just expressed.

And so, by studying these two streams in relation to each other, we find the great problem which, one can say, the historical situation posed for people at this time: the continuing reverberations of the Arthur principle, and those of the Grail principle. The problem was this: how does a human being such as Parzival, and indeed, how does Michael himself find the path from the Arthurian champions, who desire to secure Michael's dominion, to the Grail champions, who wish to forge his path into human hearts and minds so that he can grasp hold of intelligence there? And then the great problem of our own age stands clear and whole before us: Michael's new dominion obliges us to grasp hold of Christianity in a deeper sense. In the two contrasting castles—the one whose ruins we can see at Tintagel, and the other castle less easily seen by human eyes because it is surrounded by '60 leagues of impenetrable forest' on all sides—we find this problem inscribed in mighty form: how is Michael to kindle the impetus for grasping the truth of Christianity?

It would not be right to overlook the fact that the knights of King Arthur fought for Christ and in harmony with the Christ impulse. But we should remember that they still sought Christ in the sun, and did not wish to give up seeking Him there. Fighting their Michaelic battles for the Christ who works down in the rays of the sun is precisely what gave them the sense of carrying the heavens down to earth. In the Grail stream the Christ impetus worked in a quite different way, in full awareness that it had descended to earth and must be borne in human hearts, and unite the sun with human, earthly evolution. [. . .]

Extract from a lecture given in Torquay on 27 August 1924

Elaborating on the same theme, Steiner now shows how these two 'streams'—the Arthurian, nature stream and the inner Grail stream—work towards each other historically and finally meet in the ninth century, so that, as it were, picture and inner reality merge in the heart of Europe; or, one could also say, the image finds its reality and is thereby greatly enhanced and invigorated. It is from this convergence also that the Parzival epic develops in Europe, as the symbolic journey from a cosmic but naïve wisdom (Parzival is also called the 'holy fool') to a conscious grasp of the spirit in our lives and actions.

The date Steiner mentions is one he refers to elsewhere as being extremely important, for it also witnessed the ecumenical council meeting of that year at which the Church fathers, in Steiner's phrase, 'abolished the spirit'. The doctrine of the trinity of body, soul and spirit was thus replaced with a body-soul duality. Yet the Parzival saga surreptitiously works against this new, truncating doctrine in highlighting the deeds of its three prime, mutually interacting and enhancing figures, Parzival, Gawain and Feirefiz. In the penultimate section of this book we will see how these three embody essential powers of the soul.

Thus from the West working eastwards we have the Mystery of Golgotha as something legible in nature to those who could read it, as the science, we can call it, of the more highly schooled knights of the Round Table; and from the East working its way westwards we have the stream—not now legible in wind and waves, in air and water, not configured in mountains and sunshine, but instead a stream radiating through the blood of human beings and their hearts, and grasping hold of their blood—which was passing from Palestine through Greece to Italy and Spain.

And so we can say that this passes through nature on the one hand and through the blood on the other, through human hearts. These two streams move towards each other: the one that still weaves within nature, that is still present today in the whole pagan stream, bearing the pre-Christian, pagan Christ, who as sun being was spread abroad before the Mystery of Golgotha by people such as the knights of the Round Table—but also by many others. This stream also bears the pre-Christian Christ into the world during the time of the Mystery of Golgotha. And to a large extent this all emanated from the stream we can summarize as the Arthurian. One can still encounter these things today: pagan Christianity that does not directly connect with the historical event at Golgotha.

And rising to meet this is the Christianity which connects

with the Mystery of Golgotha, passing through human blood, through human hearts and souls. So we have two streams which flow towards each other: the pre-Christian Christ stream, which I will call etherealized, and the Christian Christ stream. The one later became known as the Arthur stream, while the other came to be known as the Grail stream. Both later converged: they did so within Europe and primarily also in the world of spirit.

How can we characterize this movement? The Christ who descended through the Mystery of Golgotha entered human hearts. In human hearts themselves He passed from East to West, from Palestine through Greece and Italy to Spain. Grail Christianity spread abroad through human blood, through human hearts, and Christ advanced from East to West.

This migration, as it were, was met by the spirit-ether image of the Christ coming from the West, taking its impetus from the Mystery of Golgotha but still bearing within it the Christ of the sun mysteries.

A sublime and wonderful phenomenon was unfolding here behind the scenes of world history. From the West, pagan Christianity, Arthur Christianity, which also appeared under other names and in other guises, was advancing. And from the East, Christ was passing westwards in human hearts. These two converged: the actual Christ who had descended to earth encountered His image, flowing towards Him from West to East. This convergence and encounter occurred in 869. Until this point we have clearly differentiated a stream in the North and passing through Central Europe which bore the Christ within it as sun hero—whether one called Him Baldur or some other name. Under the blazon of Christ as sun hero, the Arthurian knights spread their culture.

The other stream, inwardly rooted in the heart and later becoming the Grail stream, can be found more in the South and coming from the East, and bears the true and actual Christ within it. The stream coming from the West bears towards Him what one can call a cosmic picture.

In the ninth century, then, occurred the encounter and convergence of the Christ with Himself, with His own image: the Christ as brother of the human being and the Christ as sun hero, present only as image.

4. The Grail as Human Potential

Extract from chapter 6 of *Occult Science*, 'Present and Future Evolution of the World and Mankind'

Enhancement and conscious harmonizing of the three powers of thinking, feeling and will—closely connected with the trinity of spirit, soul and body referred to in the commentary on the previous section—is here seen as intimately connected with the Grail. Central to this enhancement are the efforts each individual makes out of himself in the course of self-development. In other words, we can see the Grail, in this sense, as the knowledge awaiting us if we can raise ourselves to it by working upon ourselves. The Grail is thus not the passive 'object' of a quest, but a potential we all bear within us.

But in the place [of ancient initiation knowledge] there developed what may be called an increasingly stronger influx into human souls of the knowledge gained through modern supersensible consciousness. The 'hidden knowledge' flows, although quite unnoticed at the beginning, into the mode of thinking of people of this period. It is self-evident that, up to the present, intellectual forces reject this knowledge. But what must happen will happen in spite of all temporary rejection. The 'hidden knowledge' which takes hold of mankind now and will take hold of it increasingly in the future, may be called symbolically 'the wisdom of the Grail'. By understanding the deeper meaning of this symbol, as it appears in legend and myth, we shall find that it is a significant image of the nature of what has been described as knowledge of the new initiation founded on the Christ mystery. Modern initiates may therefore also be called 'initiates of the Grail'. The way into the supersensible worlds, the first stages of which have been described in this book, leads to the 'science of the Grail'. [. . .] What may be known through imagination, inspiration, and intuition about higher worlds in connection with the Christ mystery will increasingly permeate humanity's life of thought, feeling, and will. The 'concealed knowledge of the Grail' will be revealed; and as an inner force it will increasingly permeate human life. [. . .]

The highest imaginable ideal of human evolution results from 'knowledge of the Grail': the spiritualization that we acquire through our own efforts. This spiritualization appears finally as a result of the harmony that we develop [. . .] between the acquired powers of intellect and feeling, and knowledge of the supersensible worlds. [. . .] The human spirit elevates itself to the tremendous impressions of its outer world and first divines and afterwards recognizes spiritual beings behind these impressions; the human heart develops a sense of the boundless sublimity of the spiritual realm.

5. Seeking for Signs of Parzival

Extract from a lecture given in Leipzig on 1 January 1914

Rather unusually, Steiner here gives a very personal account of the process of his own spiritual research into the realities underlying the Parzival legend, allowing us to accompany him on this intriguing journey of exploration. In other words, we can here witness some of the stages in his own Grail quest, and at the same time remind ourselves of some significant episodes in the saga.

Where, in this account, the hermit upbraids Parzival by reminding him of the 'mother of God', we can recall how Steiner interprets this latter figure, in the first lecture in this volume, as embodying the cleansed and purified human soul that is ready to receive the influx of spirit. Somehow there is an implication here of a connection between Parzival's lack of awareness of his mother's suffering and his failure to ask the essential, conscious and compassionate question at the Grail castle; and hence of the direction his journey must take before he fulfils his destiny.

As Steiner comes upon the name of Parzival in what he calls the 'stellar script', he presents us with a picture of the invisible spirit descending into and borne by the visible physical body, in the same way that, in the Grail saga, the host descends into the chalice on Good Friday.

[. . .] My dear friends, allow me at this point to confess to you that when in my occult researches I tried to follow this stream, I often lost trace of it; I had to search for places where it reappeared. I could suppose that the stream of the Christ impulse had reappeared slowly, and that even today it has not fully reappeared but can only give certain signs of itself. But where and how did it come to the surface? That is the question. Where did it lay hold of souls sufficiently to make an impression on their consciousness?

If you follow up the various expositions in my books and lecture courses, and if you feel about it as I do, you will find, especially in the older ones, that what I have said in connection with the name of the Holy Grail is one of the least satisfying parts. That is how I feel, and I hope that others have felt it too. It is not that I have said anything that does not hold good, but simply that when I spoke of this, I felt dissatisfied. I was confident about what I presented, but often, when I tried to trace the further course of this stream—when I tried to unravel the further occult development of Christianity in the West—then before my soul rose the admonition: 'You must first read the name of Parzival in its right place.'

I found that occult research is guided in a remarkable way. To avoid being lured into speculation, or realms where we can very easily be borne away from hidden truth on the wings of fantasy, we have to be guided slowly and by stages. Our research should ultimately bring to light a kind of self-affirming truth. So I often had to be content with waiting for an answer to the prompting: 'Search out where the name of Parzival stands!' You know from the Parzival saga that after Parzival returns, in a certain sense cured of his errors, and again finds the way to the Holy Grail, he is told that his name will appear shining upon the holy vessel. But where is this holy vessel—where is it to be found? That was the question.

In occult research of this kind one is often held back, delayed, so that one may not get very far in a day, or a year. Landmarks slowly appear. For me they appeared in the course of really a good many years, during which I sought an answer to the question—where will you find the name of Parzival written on the Holy Grail?

I knew that many meanings can be attached to the holy vessel in which the host, the holy bread or wafer, is placed. And on the holy vessel itself the name 'Parzival' was to shine. I was aware also of the deep significance of a passage such as that in St Mark's Gospel (Chapter 4, verses 11–12, and 33–34) where we are told that the Lord often spoke in parables and only gradually clarified their meaning. In occult investigation, too, one is led gradually, and very often only in connection with karmic guidance; and on encountering something that seems to have to do with a certain matter, one very often does not know what it will become in one's own soul under the influence of forces coming from the world of spirit. Often one does not know in the least whether something drawn from the depths of the esoteric world will have a bearing on some problem that one has been pursuing for years. Thus, not knowing how to proceed, I once asked the Norwegian folk spirit, the northern folk spirit, about Parzival, and he replied: 'Learn to understand the saying that through my powers *ganganda greida* flowed into the northern Parzival saga.' This means something like 'food for wayfarers' or 'journeying viaticum'.[5] I had no idea what to make of this. It was the same when I was coming out of St Peter's in Rome under the strong impression made on me by Michelangelo's *Pietà*—that you find on the right-hand side as you enter: the Mother with Jesus, the Mother who looks so young, with Jesus dead already on her knees. And after looking at this work of art (this was the kind of guidance I mean), there came to me, not as a vision but as a true imagination from the spiritual world, a picture inscribed in the Akashic record, showing how Parzival, after he first leaves the castle of the

Grail where he failed to ask about its mysteries, meets in the forest a young woman who is holding her bridegroom in her lap and weeping over him. But I knew that whether it is the mother, or the bride whose bridegroom is dead (Christ is often called the Bridegroom), the picture had a meaning, and that the connection thus established—without my having done anything about it—had a meaning also.

I could tell you of many promptings of this kind that came to me during my search for an answer to the question: where can I find the name of Parzival inscribed on the Holy Grail? For it had to be there, as the saga itself tells us. And now we need to recall the most important features of the saga.

We know that Parzival's mother, Herzeleide, bore him in great suffering and with dream-like visions of a quite peculiar character; we know that she wished to shield him from the knight's life and the code of knightly virtue; that she arranged for the management of her property and withdrew into solitude. She wanted to bring up her child as a stranger to impulses that were certainly present in him, to avoid exposing him to the dangers that had surrounded his father. But we also know that the child soon began to notice everything glorious in nature; from his mother's teaching he really learnt nothing except that there was a God in authority, and he conceived a wish to serve this God. But he knew nothing of what this God was, and when one day he met some knights he took them for God and knelt before them. When he confessed to his mother that he had seen the knights and wanted to be a knight himself, she dressed him in fool's garments and sent him on his way. He met with many adventures, and later on—people may call this sentimental but it is of the deepest significance—the mother died of a broken heart because of her son's disappearance: without turning back to give her a farewell greeting, he had set out to experience knightly adventures.

We know that after many wanderings, during which he learnt much about knightly ways and knightly honour, and distinguished himself, he came to the castle of the Grail. On other occasions I have mentioned that the best literary account of Parzival's arrival at the castle is to be found in Chrétien de Troyes. There we hear how, after frequently losing his way, Parzival comes to a lonely place and finds two men: one is steering a little boat and the other is fishing from it. They direct him to the Fisher King, and presently he encounters the latter in the Grail castle. The Fisher King is old and feeble and has to rest on a couch.

While conversing with Parzival, the Fisher King hands him a sword, a gift from his niece. Then a page carrying a spear first appears in the room: the spear is bleeding and the blood runs down over the page's hand; and then comes a maiden with the Holy Grail, which is a kind of dish. But such glory streams from it that it outshines all the lights in the hall, just as the stars are overpowered by the light of sun and moon. And then we learn how the Holy Grail contains something which nourishes the Fisher King's aged father in a separate room. He has no need of the sumptuous meal of which the Fisher King and Parzival partake. These two nourish themselves with earthly food. But each time a new course—as we should say nowadays—is served, the Holy Grail withdraws into the room of the Fisher King's aged father, whose only nourishment comes from what the Holy Grail provides.

On his way from Gurnemanz, it has been suggested to Parzival that he ought not to ask too many questions; and so he does not inquire why the lance bleeds or what the vessel of the Grail signifies—naturally he did not know their names.

He then goes to bed for the night, in the same room (according to Chrétien de Troyes) where all this has happened. He intended to ask questions in the morning, but when morning comes he finds the whole castle empty—nobody is there. He calls out but no one replies. Getting dressed and going downstairs he finds his horse ready. He thinks the whole company has ridden out to hunt and wants to ride after them to ask about the miracle of the Grail. But when crossing the drawbridge it rises up so quickly that his horse has to leap quickly over it to avoid being plunged in the castle moat. And he finds no trace of the company he encountered in the castle the previous day.

Then Chrétien de Troyes tells us how Parzival rides on and in a lonely part of the wood comes upon a woman with her husband on her knees, mourning and weeping for him. It is she, according to Chrétien de Troyes, who first suggests to him that he should have asked questions, and thus experience what effect his questions might have on the great mysteries shown him. We then hear that he goes on his way, often wandering from the right road until, precisely on a Good Friday, he comes to a hermit named Trevrizent. The hermit tells him how he is labouring under a curse for wasting the opportunity to redeem the Fisher King—which he could have done by asking questions about the miracles in the castle. And then he is given many and various teachings.

Now when I tried to accompany Parzival to the hermit, a saying was disclosed to me—a saying which, in the words my spiritual-scientific research reveals, is nowhere recorded. This was spoken—and it made a deep impression on me—by the old hermit to Parzival, after he had acquainted him as far as he could with the Mystery of Golgotha, of which Parzival knew little, although he had arrived there on a Good Friday.

The old hermit then uttered this saying (I shall use ordinary words that are perfectly faithful to the sense of the utterance): 'Think of what happened at the Mystery of Golgotha! Raise your eyes to the Christ hanging on the cross, at the moment when He said, "From this hour on, there is your mother"; and John did not leave her. But you'—said the old hermit to Parzival—'you have left your mother, Herzeleide. It was on your account that she passed from this world.'

Parzival did not fully grasp the connection, but the words were spoken with the spiritual intention that they should work in his soul as a picture, so that from this picture of John, who did not forsake his mother, he might discern the karmic debt he had incurred by deserting his own mother. This was to produce an after-effect in his soul.

We hear that Parzival stayed a short while longer with the hermit and then set out again to find the Holy Grail. And he finds the Grail shortly or directly before the death of old Amfortas, the Fisher King. Then the knights of the Holy Grail, of that holy order, approach him with the words: 'Your name shines in the Grail! You are the future ruler, the king of the Grail, for your name shines out from the holy vessel!'

Parzival becomes the Grail King. And so the name, Parzival, is inscribed on the holy, gold-gleaming vessel, which bears the host. It is inscribed there. [...]

And now, in my concern to find the vessel, I was at first misled by a certain circumstance. In occult research—I say this in all humility, with no wish to make an arrogant claim—it has always seemed to me necessary, when a serious problem is involved, to take account not only of what is drawn directly from esoteric sources, but also of what external research brings to light. And in following up a problem it seems to me specially good to make a really conscientious study of what external scholarship has to say, so that one keeps one's feet on the ground and does not get lost in cloud cuckoo land. But in the present instance exoteric scholarship led me astray (this was some time ago): I gathered from it that when Wolfram von Eschenbach began to write his Parzival poem, he had—according to his own statement—made use of Chrétien de Troyes and of a certain Kyot. External research has never been able to trace this Kyot and regards him as having been invented by Wolfram von Eschenbach, as though Wolfram von Eschenbach wanted to attribute his own extensive additions to Chrétien de Troyes to a further source. Exoteric learning is prepared to admit, at most, that Kyot was a copyist of the works of Chrétien de Troyes, and that Wolfram von Eschenbach put the whole thing together in a rather fanciful way.

So you see the direction external research takes. It is bound to draw one away, more or less, from the path that leads to Kyot. At the same time, after being somewhat led astray by external research, something else came to my attention (another instance of karmic guidance). [. . .] Today we must search among the stars in a way different from the old ways, but the stellar script must once more become something that speaks to us. These thoughts about a revival of the stellar script linked themselves in a remarkable way to the secret of Parzival, so that I could no longer avoid the conclusion that the two were connected. And then a picture rose before my soul: shown to me while I was trying to accompany Parzival in spirit on his way back to the Grail castle after his meeting with the hermit Trevrizent. Chrétien de Troyes recounts this meeting with the hermit in a particularly beautiful and touching way. I should like to read you a little from this passage, telling how Parzival comes to the hermit:

> He roused his steed to start
> And sighed from his deepest heart,
> For guilt did rack his breast,
> Remorse gave him no rest.
> Weeping he comes through the wood
> Yet halts where hermitage long has stood.
> Makes ready to dismount,
> Lays weapons on the ground—
> And finds within a chapel cell
> The pious man: before him fell
> Upon his knees in woeful plight.
> The tear that blinked before his sight
> Rolls down at last from cheek to chin
> As he with simple, childlike mien
> Folds his hands in prayer together
> In hope that he find solace here.
> —'O hear my sad confession:
> Five years I laboured in delusion
> While, poor in faith, the life I led
> Led me to many a woeful deed.'
> —'Tell me why you have so done
> And pray to God that He ere long
> Will lift you to him once again.'
> —'By Fisher King I once did stand.
> I saw the spear upon whose steel
> Hung drops of blood. I saw the Grail
> Yet failed to say the word,
> To ask the meaning of this blood;
> To ask what the Grail signified—

'Twere better I had died!
Until this day indeed
My soul's in direst need.
Our Lord I thought of never more
And from His Grace I strayed afar.'
—'Now tell me what your name may be.'
—'As Parzival men speak of me.'
The old man sighs, this name he knows
Well, very well; at last he says:
—'What you unwittingly have left undone
Has brought this sorrow upon your crown.'[6]

Then come the conversations between Parzival and the hermit of which I have spoken already. And when I sought to accompany Parzival in spirit during his return to the Grail, an image rose in the soul of how he travelled by day and night—devoting himself to nature by day and to the stars by night—as if the stellar script spoke to his unconscious self; and as if this was a prophecy of what the holy company of knights who came from the Grail to meet him would say: 'Your name shines forth in radiance from the Grail.' But Parzival, quite clearly, did not know what to make of the message of the stars, for this remained in his unconscious being, and therefore one cannot interpret it easily, however much one may try to immerse oneself in it through spiritual research.

Then I tried once more to get back to Kyot, and a particular thing which Wolfram von Eschenbach said of him made a deep impression on me, and I felt I had to relate it to the *ganganda greida*. The connection seemed inevitable. I had to relate it also to the image of the woman holding her dead bridegroom on her lap. And then, when I was not in the least looking for it, I came upon a saying attributed to Kyot: '*Er jach, ez hiez ein dinc der gral*'—'He said, a thing was called the Grail.' Now exoteric research itself tells us how Kyot came to these words '*Er jach, ez hiez ein dinc der gral*'. He acquired a book by Flegetanis in Spain—an astrological book. No doubt about it: Kyot is stimulated by Flegetanis, in whom lives a certain knowledge of the stellar script. Kyot, inspired by this revival of astrology, sees the thing called the Grail. Then I knew that I should stay close to Kyot; I knew that he discloses an important clue in a search based on spiritual science; he at least has seen the Grail.

Where, then, is the Grail, which today bears the name of Parzival? Where can it be found? In the course of my research it had become apparent that the name—that is the first thing—must be sought in the stellar script. And then, on a day which I must regard as specially significant for me, I was shown where the gold-gleaming vessel is to be found in reality, so that through it—through its symbolical expression in the stellar script—we are led to the secret of the Grail. And then I saw in the stellar script something that anyone can see—only he will not immediately discern the secret. For one day, while I was observing the gold-gleaming sickle of the moon in inner vision, as this appears in the heavens, with the dark moon like a great disc dimly visible within it, it dawned on me: with physical sight one could see the gold-gleaming moon—*ganganda greida*, the journeying viaticum—and within it the large host, the dark, wafer-like disc.[7] This is not to be seen if one merely glances superficially at the moon, but it is evident if one looks closely—and there, in wonderful letters of the occult script, was the name Parzival!

That, to begin with, was the stellar script. For in fact, if this reading of the stellar script is seen in the right light, it yields for our hearts and minds something—though perhaps not all—of the Parzival secret, the secret of the Holy Grail.

6. The Soul's Bright Vessel

Extract from a lecture given in Leipzig on 2 January 1914

In a series of resonant interconnections and correspondences, Steiner now goes on to show how we can read the image of the 'new moon with the old moon in its arms' as an emblem of the pietà: of the mother of Jesus bearing his dead body at Easter, and thus symbolically as the pure soul bearing the spirit. Yet none of this can really be grasped in intellectual concepts alone—which, like the ailing Amfortas, have no rejuvenating power. Steiner stresses the need to go beyond words and concepts into intuitive experience of and heartfelt engagement with these pictures; and suggests that this itself forms a vital part of our approach to the Grail, just as it did in Parzival's own quest.

Yesterday I tried to present what I had to tell you about the Mystery of the Grail and its connections in a way that allowed you to see how these things reveal themselves gradually to the seeker's soul. I have not withheld the various difficulties that must be gone through before the soul receives the results of research from the world of spirit. [. . .] I have for once given you this unvarnished account, because for you, as anthroposophists, it should be important to see that the results one arrives at in spiritual research are to be reached only after overcoming all the obstacles which stand in the way. And the final result of spiritual research is not the outcome of ideas that have been merely compiled; for these ideas are like messengers leading to the final result and have nothing to do with the result itself. [. . .]

I have said that the stellar script is to be found in the

heavens, but it is not in any sense the Grail itself, and it does not yield us the Grail. I have expressly emphasized—and I beg you to take this very seriously—that the name of the Grail, not the Grail itself, is to be found in the stellar script. I have pointed to the fact that in the gold-gleaming sickle of the moon—as any close observer can see—the dark part of the moon emerges and is as though delineated from the bright sickle; and there, in occult writing, the name of Parzival is to be found.

Now before we go further and try to interpret this sign in the heavens, I must draw your attention to an important law, an important fact. The gold-gleaming sickle becomes apparent because the physical rays of the sun fall on the moon. The illuminated part of the moon shines out as the gleaming vessel, and within it rests the dark host: in physical terms, this is the dark part where the sun's rays do not fall; spiritually, there is something else. When the rays of the sun fall on part of the moon and are reflected in gleaming light, something nevertheless passes through its physical matter. This something is the spiritual element that lives in the sun's rays. The spiritual power of the sun is not held back and reflected, as the sun's physical power is, but passes through; and because of the moon's resistance, what we see at rest, contained as a disc in the golden vessel, is actually the spiritual power of the sun. So we can say that in the dark part of the moon we are looking at the spiritual power of the sun. In the gold-gleaming part, the vessel, we see reflected the physical power of the sun. The spirit of the sun rests within the vessel of the sun's physical power. So in truth the spirit of the sun rests in the vessel of the moon. And if we now recollect all that we have ever said about this sun spirit in relation to Christ, then what the moon does physically embodies an important symbol. Because the moon reflects the sun's rays and in this way brings into being the gold-gleaming vessel, it appears to us as the bearer of the sun spirit, for the latter appears within the moon's vessel in the form of the wafer-like disc.

And let us remember in the Parzival saga how the host descends from heaven into the Grail and is renewed every Good Friday—thus during the Easter festival. It sinks into the Grail like a rejuvenating nourishment at the Easter festival, when the hermit directs Parzival towards the Grail; at the Easter festival, whose significance for the Grail Wagner's *Parsifal* has again brought close to us.

Now let us recall how the date of the Easter festival was established in accordance with an old tradition—one of those traditions I mentioned yesterday as arising from the working of the Christ impulse in the depths of the soul. What day is assigned to the Easter festival? The day when the vernal sun, which means the sun that is gathering strength—our symbol for the Christ—reaches the first Sunday after the full moon. How does the vernal full moon stand in the heavens at the Easter festival—how must it stand? It starts, if only a little, to form a sickle. Something must be visible of the dark part; something of the sun spirit who has gained his vernal strength must be contained within it. This means that, according to an ancient tradition, the picture of the Holy Grail must appear in the heavens at the Easter festival. It must be so. At the Easter festival, therefore, everyone can see this picture of the Holy Grail. According to a very ancient tradition, the date of the Easter festival is regulated with this in view. [...]

And if we now ask how Parzival gradually gains knowledge, what do we find? Who is he, this Parzival? He is ignorant of certain things; he is held to be ignorant—but of what? Now we have heard that the Christ impulse flows on as though through subterranean channels in the depths of the soul. Up above, in conscious debate, the theological controversies go on, and from them traditional Christianity takes shape. Let us follow the personality of Parzival, as the saga portrays him. He knows nothing about the superficial course of events; he is kept in ignorance of all that. He is protected from it. What he learns to know comes from sources active in the depths of the soul, as we heard yesterday. At first, riding away in ignorance from the Grail castle, he learns it from the woman who mourns the dead bridegroom in her lap; then from the hermit with mystic powers; and from the power of the Grail, for it is on a Good Friday that he comes to the hermit; and so already the power of the Grail is working in him unconsciously. Thus he is one of those who know nothing of what has been going on externally but who are led to meet the new age through influences flowing from unconscious sources. He is a man whose heart and soul could receive the secret of the Grail in innocence, undisturbed by the effects of the external world on human life. He is to receive the secret with the highest, purest, noblest forces of the soul. He has to meet someone who has not developed the soul forces which could fully experience the Grail: he has to meet Amfortas. While Amfortas was indeed marked out as the guardian of the Grail, he succumbed to the lower forces in human nature. And how he succumbed is connected with the guardianship of the Grail: he killed his adversary out of lust and jealousy. [...] Worldly concerns could be approached with earthly forces, but it was not permitted to approach the concerns of the Holy Grail in this way, as Amfortas discovered. Anyone attempting it was bound to suffer pain. And since the workings of the stars had been permeated by Christ, a man was needed who had remained untouched by controversies in the external world and whose karma enabled Christ to draw near to his soul. Parzival, in whom the Christ power was still working unconsciously, arrives [...]; and the wound [of Amfortas] burns as it had never burned before.

Thus we see how the new age declares itself; how the soul of Parzival is related to the new, subconscious, historical impulse permeated by the Christ aura, the Christ impulse, although he knows nothing of it. But the forces which had guided human history from below the surface were gradually to emerge; and Parzival, accordingly, had to come by degrees to understand something that will never be understood unless it is approached with the pure and blameless forces of the soul, and not with traditional knowledge and scholarship. [...]

Let us vividly imagine the virgin mother with the Christ upon her knees and let us then express it thus: Whoever can feel the holiness of this picture will feel the same for the Holy Grail. Above all other lights, all other gods, shines the holy vessel—the moon-mother now touched by Christ, the new Eve, the bearer of the sun-spirit Christ.

Think of the 'what', but still more of the 'how'! And let us look into the soul of Parzival: how, riding out from the Grail castle, he encounters the sight of the bride and bridegroom, which brings him into connection with subconscious Christ forces. Let us look at how the hermit at Eastertide, when the picture of the Grail is written in the heavens, in the stellar script, gives instruction to Parzival's pure soul. Let us follow him as he rides on—as I emphasized yesterday—by day and night, looking at nature by day and with the symbol of the Holy Grail often before him at night; how he rides on with the gold-gleaming sickle of the moon before him: with the host, the Christ spirit, the sun spirit within it. Let us see how, on this journey, the correlation between the picture of the virgin mother with her bridegroom son and the sign of the heavenly script prepares him to understand the secret of the Holy Grail.

Let us see how permeation of the earth's destiny by the Christ impulse works together in Parzival's soul with the stellar script which has to be renewed; let us see how all that is permeated with Christ is related to the forces of the stars. [. . .]

The Grail cannot in fact be approached through words of any kind, or through philosophical speculations. The only way to approach it is by changing all these words into feeling, by becoming able to feel in the Grail the sum of all that is holy, by feeling that what was carried over from the Moon period of planetary evolution,[8] appearing first in the earth mother, Eve, and then in renewed form in the virgin mother [. . .] flows together into the coming of the Christ being, who poured Himself into the earth's aura and became the new Lord of the earth. We approach it by feeling the confluence of what works down from the stars, and is symbolized in the stellar script, with human evolution on earth. If one takes all this into account and feels it as the consonance of human history with the stellar script, then one also grasps the secret expressed in the words entrusted to Parzival in the saga: that whenever a king of the Grail, a truly appointed guardian of the Grail, dies, the name of his accredited successor appears on the Holy Grail. 'There it is to be read'—which means that it will be necessary to learn to read the stellar script again in a new form.

Let us try to make ourselves worthy to do this; let us try to read the stellar script in the form now given to us. For in fact it is nothing other than a reading of the script when we try to trace human evolution through the Saturn, Sun and Moon periods of evolution, right up to the Vulcan period.[9] But we must recognize the context in which we wish to decipher the stellar script today. Let us make ourselves worthy of it! It is far from insignificant when we hear that the Grail was at first taken from its proper location and for a season was not externally perceptible. Let us regard our studies of anthroposophy as a renewed search for the Grail, and let us try to learn to understand the meaning of what formerly spoke from subconscious depths of soul, then rose gradually into human consciousness. Let us try to transform this by degrees into a new and more conscious language! Let us try to explore a wisdom which will disclose to us the connection between the earthly and the heavenly, not relying on old traditions, but in the way in which it can be revealed today. [...]

III

THE QUEST AND THE QUESTION: PIERCING THROUGH MATERIALISM

7. The Questioning Stance of Soul

Extract from a lecture given in Berlin on 6 January 1914

The relationship between questions and answers can be resolved in a number of ways, for instance by a refusal to countenance the uncertainties of doubt, and pressing on instead to an answer at all costs; or, more uncomfortably, by choosing to seek patiently in the space that opens up between them, 'entertaining' doubts and allowing their resolution through a slow process of growth and increasing understanding. Here, in connection with Parzival's failure to ask the right question at the Grail castle, Steiner discusses the differences between a more materialistic or more spiritual stance of soul in relation to questions and answers. Rilke once wrote: 'Be patient towards all that is unresolved in your heart and try to love the questions themselves ... live the questions now. Perhaps you will gradually, without noticing it, live at last some distant day into the answers.'[10] *Materialism, suggests Steiner, is unwilling to pose the really fundamental questions because it thinks it has all the answers already.*

In the first place we have to consider how Parzival, several centuries after the Mystery of Golgotha, marks an important step in the working of the Christ event in a human soul.

Parzival was the son of a knight-errant and the lady Herzeleide. The knight departed before Parzival was even born, leaving his mother to suffer pain and torment before he ever arrived on earth. She wanted to protect her son from everything connected with knightly virtues and from developing one's powers by being a knight. She brought him up in such a way that he knew nothing of the outside world or of what it might offer. He grew up in isolation in the wilds of nature, knowing only what nature could teach. His mother wanted him to know nothing of what normally unfolds between knights and amongst other people. The story even relates that he knew nothing of the religious ideas current in the world. His mother told him only that God exists and underlies everything. He wished to serve God, but he knew no more than this: that he might serve God. Everything else was kept hidden from him. However, the urge to be a knight[11] was so powerful that one day he felt urged to leave his mother, and set forth into the world to seek his destiny. After many wanderings he came to the Grail castle. The best description of what happened there—in relation to what we can gather from the spiritual record of these events—is found in Chrétien de Troyes,[12] who was also a source for Wolfram von Eschenbach's *Parzival.*[13] We learn that in his wanderings, Parzival one day arrived at a wooded region by a shore where two men were fishing. At his request they showed him the way to the castle of the Fisher King. On reaching the castle he entered and saw a weak, sick man lying on a couch. The man gave him a sword, that of his niece. Parzival also saw a squire enter with a lance from which blood was dripping onto the squire's hands. Then a maiden carrying a golden chalice entered, the light from which shone brighter than all other lights in the hall. A meal was served. Each time another course was served, the chalice was carried past Parzival into the next room, where the Fisher King's father was nourished by it.

To Parzival all this seemed a marvel; but earlier on in his wanderings, a knight had advised him not to ask many questions. He therefore did not ask about what he saw here, though he intended to the following morning. Yet when he woke the next day, the castle was deserted. He called out but no one came. He thought the knights had gone hunting and wanted to follow them. In the castle yard he found his horse saddled and ready. He rode off but had to be quick to get over the drawbridge: his horse had to leap the gap when the drawbridge was pulled up as he rode over it. He saw no sign of the knights however.

Of course we know what this was about: Parzival had not asked the question he should have. The most wondrous thing appeared before him, but he asked nothing. He was repeatedly told that part of his mission was to ask about the wondrous things he encountered. When he did not ask, it slowly dawned on him that this failure had caused a kind of ill fate. Thus we see an individual brought up in isolation from the culture of the world, supposed to know nothing about it, who was meant to ask about the mysteries of the Grail when these came before him: but to ask in a virginal way, as a soul not affected or influenced by the culture of the day. Why was he to ask in this way? I have suggested on a number of occasions that the Christ impulse led to a deed that humanity was not immediately able to understand. On the one hand, therefore, the fact that the Christ had streamed into the aura of the earth has had an ongoing effect irrespective of what people might think or contend in all kinds of theological dogmas—it went on working regardless. And the western world took shape under the influence of this Christ impulse, which may be said to have worked on human souls at a profound level, behind the scenes of history. If this impulse had acted only insofar as people understood it and disputed about it, it would not have contributed much to human evolution. But at the time of Parzival an important moment came when the Christ impulse had to be taken one step further.

Parzival was therefore not meant to learn of the sacrifice by Christ at Golgotha, nor what the Apostles, the Church fathers and others later taught in different theological streams. He was not meant to know how knights put themselves and their virtues at the service of Christ. He was meant only to be in touch with the Christ impulse deep down in his soul to the extent that this was possible at the time. His connection with this would have been clouded if he had learned doctrinal teachings about the Christ. The Christ impulse works less in what people do or say than in the soul's experience when it is given up wholly to this supersensible influence. That was to be the case with Parzival. Outward teachings always belong to the sense world. The Christ impulse works at a level beyond the senses and was intended to influence Parzival's soul at that level. The one and only thing he was meant to do was to ask his question in the place where the significance of the Christ impulse could be revealed, at the Grail castle. His question was to be invoked not by the reverence which the knights believed they owed Christ, nor by the reverence theologians believed they owed Christ, but simply by the fact that his soul was virginal, though in tune with the time in which he lived. He was to ask what the Grail might reveal, and indeed, what the Christ event might mean for humanity. He was meant to ask! Let us keep this in mind.

There was someone else in history who, in contrast, was *not* meant to ask. The story is well known. It was the undoing of the young man at Sais[14] that he felt compelled to ask, doing what he was not meant to do, and wishing to see the image of Isis unveiled. This man was the equivalent of Parzival before the Mystery of Golgotha. Then, however, the young man was told: 'Take care lest your soul is unprepared when what lies behind the veil is revealed!' Parzival is 'the young man at Sais' after the Mystery of Golgotha. He was not to receive any special preparation but was to be guided to the Grail with his soul still virginal. He failed to do the most important thing, not asking or seeking to have the mystery unveiled to his soul. That is how times have changed in humanity's evolution. [. . .]

When Parzival rode away from the castle, having failed to ask about the mysteries of the Grail, a woman, a bride mourning her newly dead bridegroom lying across her knees, was among the first people he met. This is the image of the mother mourning her son, the very familiar pietà theme. It gives a hint of what Parzival would have learned if he had asked his question. He would have learned of the connection between Isis and her son Horus in its new form, the connection between the mother and the Son of Man. And he should have asked the question!

Here we see a profound indication of the progress made in the course of human evolution. Something that must not happen before the Mystery of Golgotha ought to happen after it, for humanity has meanwhile progressed: the soul of humanity has changed. [. . .] The fruit to be gained from the Parzival mystery, augmented by the image of the young man of Sais, is that we learn to ask questions in a way that accords with our times. Learning to ask questions is to follow the upward stream in human evolution.

After the Mystery of Golgotha we have essentially two streams in human evolution: one that holds to the Christ impulse and gradually takes us to the heights of spirit, and one that represents a continuation of the descent into materialism. Today these two streams are muddled to the extent that our civilization is very largely tainted by the materialistic stream. We must therefore look without bias or prejudice at everything the science of the spirit can tell us of the Christ impulse and everything connected with it, so that we may realize that the soul needs inner, spiritual development to balance an external world that is inevitably becoming ever more materialistic. We must see from aspects such as those presented here that we have to learn to ask questions.

We must learn to ask questions in the spiritual stream. In the materialistic stream everything is designed to stop people asking questions. Let us consider the two side by side to get a clear picture of their nature. On the one hand we have people who are materialists—which does not mean they don't subscribe to various spiritual dogmas, theoretically acknowledging the world of spirit or paying lip-service to it. But that is not what matters. What matters is that our souls enter wholly into the spiritual stream. Those in the materialistic stream may be said to be people who do not ask questions, for they know it all already. It is a characteristic feature of materialism that such people know everything and do not wish to ask questions. Even the very young know everything today and do not ask questions. It is felt that people are free and their value as individuals enhanced if they can always form their own opinions. But the problem is: how does this personal opinion develop? We grow into being a part of the world. With the first words we hear as children we take something in. We continue to grow, absorbing more and more, not realizing how we absorb things. Our karma has made us who we are, and because of this we like some things more and others less. We grow up, forming our opinions, and reach, say, the age of 25—which many believe to be a perfectly respectable age for forming one's own opinions. We feel our judgement to be mature, believing it is our own. Yet anyone who can see into souls knows that this judgement is based on nothing more than the external life in which we find ourselves, which has come into focus in our own soul. We may even find ourselves in inner conflict because our judgement suggests to us that we should take a particular path. Believing ourselves to be independent, we become all the more slavishly dependent on our own inner life. We form opinions but are completely unable to ask questions.

We only learn to ask questions when we can develop the inner poise and harmony that allows reverence and devotion to be retained towards sacred spheres of life; and when we can retain in ourselves an element that always seeks to remain independent even of our own judgement in relation to what approaches us from these spheres. We only learn to ask questions by developing a mood of expectancy that allows life to reveal something to us; by being able to wait; by feeling some hesitation in applying our own judgement, especially in relation to anything that should flow in a sacred way from the sacred spheres of existence; by not judging but asking questions, not only of people who may be able to reply, but above all of the world of spirit. We should look towards that world not with our formed opinions but with our questions: in a questioning mood and attitude.

Try to get a really clear understanding through meditation of the difference between meeting the spiritual aspects of life with opinions or meeting them with questions. You have to experience the radical difference between the two. This difference is connected with an aspect of our modern age that requires special attention. Our spiritual stream can only grow and develop if we learn to see the difference between questions and opinions. Of course we have to use our judgement in daily life; and I do not suggest for a moment that we should be wary of using it in all daily situations. No, it is in relation to the deeper secrets of the world that we must learn to develop an expectant, questioning mood. Our spiritual movement will progress through anything that acknowledges and cultivates that mood in a relatively large proportion of the human race. It will be inhibited by anything that counters the spiritual stream in the form of unconsidered opinions. If, at truly solemn moments in life, we try to reflect on what we can gain from a story such as that of Parzival, who was meant to ask questions when he went to the Grail castle, the story can become an example to us in our movement. And many other things will become clear in connection with this. [. . .]

Ancient clairvoyance had vanished by the fourth post-Atlantean epoch, which is when the Mystery of Golgotha took place. The human soul assumed a different organization which meant that the world of spirit must remain closed to it unless it developed the urge to ask questions. The powers harmful to the human soul in older times cannot touch it now if it enquires into the secret of the Grail. This secret concerns the element that has flowed into the earth's aura since the Mystery of Golgotha. What had not previously flowed into it, but then did and does, would remain forever unknown unless we ask. We must ask questions—which means that we must feel the urge to let an element already inherent in the soul truly develop. [. . .]

Since the Mystery of Golgotha, someone who begins to ask questions will be able to find the right way of doing so, and will also get the right feeling for the new Isis Mystery. What matters today, then, is to ask the right questions, and develop the right attitude to the spiritual world view that can now be presented. Someone who merely wishes to judge can read any number of books and lectures without learning anything apart from mere words. Someone, on the other hand, who approaches in a questing mood, will learn far more than can be found in the words. He will find that these words bear fruit in the powers of growth that lie in his own soul. Anything the spirit teaches us must become real inner experience. That is the important thing. [. . .]

8. The Lapse into Matter

Extract from a lecture given in Dornach on 16 April 1921

When Steiner says here that 'we still are and should be seekers for the Holy Grail', he is suggesting that this quest is now even more essential than it was in the medieval period when the saga arose. It is easy to see how spiritual endeavours for apparently intangible goals can 'fall back' as it were into the search for merely physical realities. This is something we repeatedly encounter—just to take one example, in modern forms of education that often place value on quantifiable achievements at the expense of the unfolding of a child's still unknown (and therefore invisible and immeasurable) gifts and potential. Steiner's own examples here are the realms of astronomy and medicine, which materialistic outlooks have burdened with loss of transformative or healing perception.

Wolfram von Eschenbach ... was spared the dogmatism [that gripped Europe in the twelfth and thirteenth centuries]. Those who raised this call for the Holy Grail meant to let it resound in the spirit of freedom dawning in dull souls. They did not wish to deprive the human being of his freedom nor impose anything on him. He was to be one who questioned. Out of the depths of his own soul he was to ask about the miracles of the Holy Grail. [...]

When the spiritual path of the servants of the Grail was superseded by the earthly path of the journey to the physical Jerusalem in the East—when, in other words, the quest for the Grail was replaced by crusades to an earthly Jerusalem [...] this was the translation into something materialistic of what the servants of the Holy Grail had intended to be spiritual.

This, too, was one of the paths materialism led to—leading to the physical not the spiritual Jerusalem. The spiritual Jerusalem was said to enshrine in Titurel's temple what remained of the Mystery of Golgotha as the Holy Grail. Legend held that Titurel had brought this Holy Grail down to the earth's sphere from the clouds where it hovered, borne up by angels during the age of Arabism and the prosaic narration of the events in Palestine. The age of materialism, however, did not start asking about the Holy Grail. Isolated individuals, who did not participate in the general wisdom of the age but dwelled in a kind of stupor, like Parzival, were the ones who set out to seek the Holy Grail. But they also did not understand how to ask the proper, relevant question. Thus the path of materialism which began in the first third of the fourteenth century, was preceded by that other path of materialism already expressed in the turn to the East, the eastward journey to the physical Jerusalem. Modern humanity experienced this tragedy, and human beings had to and still have to undergo it, to comprehend themselves inwardly and to become people who really ask questions. Modern humanity had to and still has to experience the tragedy that the light that once approached from the East was not recognized as spiritual light. Spiritual light was rejected, and instead people set out to find a physical location in the East. In the Middle Ages humanity began to seek the physical East after the spiritual East was rejected at the close of antiquity.

Such then was the situation in Europe; and our age today is still a part of it, for if we understand the true inner call resounding in human hearts we still are and should be seekers for the Holy Grail. The endeavours of humanity that started with the crusades still await their metamorphosis into spiritual endeavours. We have yet to arrive at an understanding of cosmic worlds that allows us to seek Christ there. As long as the cosmos is investigated only through external, physical astronomy, it naturally cannot be seen as the home of Christ. The Christ could not have descended to earth to incarnate in the human being Jesus of Nazareth from the cosmos of the modern astronomer, which he describes only by means of geometry, mathematics and mechanics. Nor can this incarnation be understood through knowledge of the physical nature of the human being derived by moving away from living people to the corpse dissected for research purposes—thus giving rise to views about the living human being based on the dead corpse.

In antiquity, people possessed an astronomy imbued with life, and medical knowledge was likewise imbued. Our quest must once again be for a living astronomy, a living medicine. Just as a living astronomy will reveal to us a heaven, a cosmos that is truly pervaded by spirituality, from which Christ could descend, so an enlivened medicine will show us the human being in a way that enables us to penetrate with insight and understanding to the mystery of the blood, to the organic inner sphere where the forces of the etheric body, the astral body and the I transform themselves into the physical blood. When true medical knowledge has grasped the mysteries of the blood, and spiritualized astronomy has understood the cosmic spheres, we shall understand how it was possible for the Christ to descend from cosmic spheres to the earth; how He could find on earth the human body that could receive Him with its blood. The mystery of the Grail must be sought in this way in all earnestness: by embarking on the path to the spiritual Jerusalem with all that we are as human beings, with powers of both head and heart. This really is the task of modern humanity.

It is strange how the essence of what ought to come into being weaves objectively through the world's fabric. If it is not perceived in the right way, it is experienced outwardly instead, becomes superficially materialized. The flocking of people to Jerusalem expresses yet another phase of materialism, indicating how something that ought to be understood spiritually by all modern humanity is interpreted only in a more materialistic way. The time must come when the mystery of the Grail will once again be understood in the right way. [. . .]

9. Piercing the Thicket

Extract from a lecture given in Dornach on 17 April 1921

The castle of the Holy Grail, or 'Mont Salvat' (mountain of healing or redemption) was said to be surrounded by impenetrable, impassable terrain—a metaphor perhaps for the lifelong quest to penetrate the thickets of a materialistic view of the world that mostly surrounds us today. Yet the necessary difficulty of the endeavour is also what enables us to develop the strength to accomplish it, a paradox that Steiner hints at here. One meaning of the name Parzival, as we have seen, is to 'pierce through the valley'—which might also be the valley of the shadow of death: to pierce through it very actively to a different kind of perception—a word which itself seems closely related to the hero of this saga.

[. . .] Only a few individuals could indicate that the impulse of Christianity was once couched in oriental wisdom, and that what contained this oriental view, the sacred vessel of the Grail, could be brought to Europe by means of divine spirits who hovered above the earth, bearing it. Only then, they said, was a hidden castle built for it, the Grail castle on Mont Salvat. It was also said that one could only approach the miracles of the Holy Grail by traversing inaccessible regions. These sages did not say that the impassable region surrounding the castle was 60 miles in breadth, but put it in a much more esoteric way. They said: 'Oh, these Europeans cannot reach the Holy Grail, for the path they must take to get there is as long as the path from birth to death. Only when human beings arrive at the portal of death, having trod the path impassable for

Europeans, extending from birth to death, will they arrive at the Grail castle on Mont Salvat.'

This was, basically, the esoteric secret conveyed to pupils. Since the time had not yet arrived when human beings could discern with clear perception how a world of spirit might once again be discovered, these pupils were told they could enter the sacred castle of the Grail only by way of occasional glimpses of light. In particular they were given strict injunctions that they had to *ask*, that the time had arrived in human evolution when those who do not ask—who do not develop their own inner being and do not seek the impulse of truth on their own but remain passive—cannot arrive at an experience of themselves. The I must be discovered through our physical organization. This self-discovering I must in turn raise itself up by its own power in order to behold itself where, even in early Greek culture, the self was still beheld: in supersensible worlds. The I must first raise itself to perception of itself as something supersensible. [...]

Human beings must learn to understand why an impassable region surrounds the castle of the Grail, why the path between birth and death is difficult terrain. When they understand why it is difficult, when they grasp that the I experiences itself through the physical organization, when they sense how impossible merely physical astronomy and medicine are, then they themselves will clear the paths and smooth the way. Then people will bring into this hitherto arduous terrain between birth and death what comes into being through their own inner efforts.

Out of the substance of soul and spirit, human beings have to fashion the tools with which to plough a way, the soul-way leading to the castle of the Grail, to the mystery of the Grail, to the mystery of bread and blood, to the fulfilment of the words 'This do in remembrance of me'.[15] This is, truly, done in remembrance of the mighty event of Golgotha, if the symbol of the bread—of what, in other words, develops from the earth through the synthesis of cosmic forces—is understood. It is done in full remembrance if we understand once again how to grasp the world through a spiritualized cosmology and astronomy, and if we learn to comprehend the human being in terms of his essence: the element where the spiritual directly enters him—the mystery of the blood. The path that leads to the Holy Grail must be found through inner work in human souls. This is the task of cognition and the social task. It is also one to which people are extremely antagonistic today.

Because people are embedded in western civilization's ego-accentuating culture and education they develop a longing, above all, to remain inwardly passive, and not to allow earthly existence to give them what could help their souls progress. Taking active hold of soul forces, inward experience in general—not necessarily esoteric development but inner experience in general—is something people in Europe do not much care for. They prefer to perpetuate what was natural in a preceding era, that is, ego development, potentially leading to the most blatant egotism, to the blindest raging of instincts when it outlives its proper time. This ego sense, extending beyond the time properly assigned to it, has firstly given rise to nationalistic sentiments and appears in national chauvinism. Such feelings engender minds who wish to keep the path to the Holy Grail impassable. But it is our obligation to do everything possible to invoke human activity in the areas both of knowledge and the social sphere. All the forces pervaded by hatred of inward soul activity emerge in opposition to such a call. People have, after all, been conditioned for long enough to conclude that any efforts they make to free themselves from guilt must be heretical. They think they should cultivate a proper awareness of sin and guilt, that they should not advance through their own efforts but should be redeemed by Christ, in passivity.

We fail to understand Christ if we do not acknowledge Him as the cosmic power that unites with us completely when we work our way through to Him through questions and inner activity. Today, everywhere, we see powers that seek to obstruct the path of inner activity—religious creeds and theological doctrines, military power and science. I have been calling attention to this for a long time, and again and again have had to say that these powers of opposition will become increasingly vehement. One really cannot say at all that such opposition has reached its peak yet, not by a long way. It has a strong organizing power in focusing all the elements that, though destined to wane, can, in their very waning, obstruct for the time being all that supports upward-striving forces. The forces nurturing inner soul activity are weak today in comparison with the opposing elements. The powers are weak that try to inwardly acquire progressive forces. The world has assumed an ahrimanic character:[16] for it was inevitable that the I, having encountered and comprehended itself in the physical sphere, is seized hold of by ahrimanic forces if it remains in the physical sphere and does not raise itself again, in due course, to a spiritual understanding of itself as spiritual being. We can see this process of usurpation by ahrimanic powers; we can observe it in a real tendency towards evil that is making itself felt today—little as sleepy souls are willing to admit this. [. . .]

If the human being is to come to anthroposophy through

his own judgement, he must become one who asks questions; he must convince himself through his innermost freedom of judgement. He may hear words of spiritual truth but convincing himself of it is something he has to do on his own. If he wishes to participate and be active in society and the community he must do so out of his innermost heart impulses. Those who most truly take up anthroposophical spiritual science must become people who ask questions. [. . .]

IV

NEW SPIRITUAL COMMUNITY: THE GRAIL AS TRANSFORMED LARYNX

10. The Living Word

Extract from a lecture given in Berlin on 1 April 1907

In this passage we first meet the astonishing idea that humanity will one day advance far enough into selfless mastery of life forces to be able to create new beings through the power of the spoken Word. The Word that originally created all things will then have matured within us to the point where we become co-creators with the divine. At the same time this is intimately connected with overcoming the matter-bound experiences of sexuality and egotism; of enhancing our separate individuality to the point where we can reconnect consciously with all other beings in a new, higher community. This overcoming of narrow ties of blood and race is prefigured in the unifying experience of Whitsun, when the disciples are able suddenly to speak to all 'in their own language'. Though there is no specific mention of the Grail here, in subsequent passages in this section Steiner expressly connects mastery of life forces with the Grail's healing, nourishing and unifying potency.

[...] Until Jesus Christ appeared on the earth, Christ's spiritual presence was a unity. It was a uniform sheath surrounding the entire earth, with its 'skeleton' in the earth. If you take the solid earth and all that is within it, and add the warmth around the earth, you have more or less what is called the body of the Christ spirit. Hence the beautiful words in St John's gospel where Jesus Christ calls Himself the spirit of the earth: 'Those who eat my bread tread on me with their feet.' (John 13:18). Don't human beings eat bread? The bread they eat is the body of Christ. When they walk on the earth they step on him with their feet. This should be taken literally.

In the Lemurian age,[17] the spirit of Yahweh, the element of the spirit, was gradually poured into individual human beings; similarly, the Christ spirit, whose body is in the warmth of the blood, poured Himself slowly into human beings during the ages preceding and following Jesus Christ. When the entire spirit of Christ has been poured into human individuals, then Christianity (that is, the great community of humanity) will have appropriated the earth. There will no longer be any consciousness of clans and blood relations whatsoever, but only an awareness of humanity as a community. Despite the greatest individualization, every individual will be drawn to every other. Small tribal and ethnic communities will give way to the community of life-spirit, buddhi, the community of Christ.

To a clairvoyant eye of soul gazing down upon our planet, the Christ spirit would once have been seen as fully contained in what surrounds the earth, and then would be seen pouring into human individuals. Different colours and moods would be seen arising, and what once surrounded the earth would then have to be sought within individual human beings. This is the cosmic significance of the appearance of Jesus Christ. [...]

The original outpouring of the spirit caused love to be bound to the blood. The people of ancient times who lived in small, tribal communities did not love one another any less than people do today. Indeed, they loved one another more, but their love was like that of a mother for her child, conditioned more by nature. Blood itself was attracted to blood and the human feeling of belonging together was expressed in that blood attraction. As humanity developed however, people began to feel sympathy for one another as individuals. In this way, smaller groups, families and communities developed, then together formed larger communities. As individuals, however, human beings became increasingly egotistic and self-seeking. On the one hand, therefore, we have human beings becoming increasingly self-seeking, and on the other the arrival of the unifying influence of Christ: increasing individuation and independence along with the unifying spirit of Christianity. Only when both these streams have perfected themselves will it be possible to manifest a condition on earth in which everyone is independent and, at the same time, connected with one another through being permeated with the Christ spirit.

We must realize that all this is connected with the blood: that originally something was expressed in the blood that was revealed in human feelings and worked within blood relationships to bring about love of family. Then human beings became increasingly egotistic. Self-seeking entered increasingly into the blood. This is the secret of human evolution, that the blood assumed a self-seeking character. This blood, grown egotistic, had to be overcome. The excessive egotism in human blood was sacrificed, actually flowed in a mystical yet real way from the wounds of Jesus Christ on the cross. Had this blood not flowed, the self-seeking element of human blood would have grown ever greater throughout evolution. The Mystery of Golgotha purified the blood of self-seeking. Through this profound love, human blood was saved from its self-seeking.

The cosmic significance of what happened at Golgotha cannot be understood by someone who sees only that a human being hung on the cross and bled when pierced by a spear. The deep mystical significance of this process lies in the fact that His blood represented the blood that humankind had to lose for its salvation. No one can understand Christianity who interprets these things materialistically, who knows only the physical, material events without the spiritual background. This spiritual background is the regenerating effect of the blood of the Saviour that flowed on the cross. We can understand the further evolution of humanity only if we grasp just how decisive this fact is, only if we can comprehend that the mightiest revolution in the spiritual evolution of humanity on earth is connected with this fact. [. . .]

This points to the future of human evolution on earth. All that is base and inferior in the human being will fall away. What the human being will later become is already being prepared within him. Human beings will no longer be creative, as today, out of their lower passions. We will become increasingly creative in the way that today we utter the Word, incarnating the most sublime things. Just as human beings have become more egotistic through sexuality, so through the falling away of sexuality we will become selfless again. The Word we bring forth today in a stream of air from the larynx will in future be able to create humankind. The voice changes at puberty. The voice will come to be the reproductive power. At the same time this Word (because the relationship will be entirely reversed in future) will express human mastery of the air. The breath originally blowing through the human being like the wind, will work to transform something connected with us at an even deeper level. The Word will become creative enough to purify and clean the blood. Even human blood will be transformed and become capable of invoking only pure, selfless feelings. There will be but a single human race, creative through the Word. Selflessness will become a characteristic of the blood and the heart will become the organ of thinking. The age represented by Judas Iscariot is ruled by egotism. Anyone who observes world events with an unprejudiced eye can see how sexuality in human beings is in a position to betray and crush them as spirits. Nevertheless, when the heart becomes the organ for spiritual perception, human beings will one day create through the Word just as, today, they produce the Word as something higher than themselves.

I ask you now to apply this to the Gospel and to consider a scene where this is wonderfully expressed with majestic symbolism. Look at what will happen when Christianity becomes selfless and brotherly; consider how what makes us egotistic is incarnated in Judas Iscariot, and look at what human beings are developing towards, through 12 stages, to the form that Jesus Christ Himself assumed. Everything rises to the heart.

The transformation takes place in such a way that the creative power rises from the lap to the heart. This must be expressed in the one who embodies the noblest figure and who is closest to Jesus. We read: 'One of his disciples, whom Jesus loved, was reclining in the lap (*kolpos*) of Jesus. So Peter beckoned to him that he might inquire who it might be. So, lying close to the breast of Jesus, he said to him, "Lord, who is it?"' (John 13:33). This scene shows how the lowest forces of human creation are lifted into the breast, portrayed by the most intimate of Jesus Christ's disciples. The mystery of the Son, of Jesus, is indicated here with great subtlety. [. . .]

The Last Supper was a preparation for what was then to take place on the physical plane. For this reason we can learn from Christ's death the overcoming of death on the physical plane, the overcoming of egotistic blood by the flow of blood from the wounds. We also come to know the majestic perspective revealed when these words resound from the cross out of a consciousness of the future: the earth has attained the goal of complete community, the spiritualization, the overcoming of everything that can drag down the human spirit.

Those who undergo this by the side of Christ will be able to gather around Him when they depart from earthly evolution and rise to a higher evolution. Jesus Christ will be able to call out once again, at the conclusion of earth's perfecting, the words he uttered from the cross: '*Eli, eli, lama sabachthani!*' 'My God, my God, how you have glorified, spiritualized the I within humanity.' That is what these words mean [. . .]:[18] 'My God, my God, how powerfully, how much, you have glorified and spiritualized me!'

These words reveal to us the spirit's struggle to free itself from the body. The mystery of the Son reveals that the world's Saviour's inner vision saw to the end of the earth's perfecting. He expressed the great goal of humanity in these words concerning the overcoming of all differences and the establishing of the greatest love of humankind. This goal can be achieved only when all human beings learn to enter the world of spirit, for the unification of humankind lies in the spirit. Human beings were once one when they emerged from the all-flowing godhead. They were then individualized through their descent into individual human bodies, much the way that water becomes individualized when absorbed by tiny sponges. In the future, these individualized human beings will again be unified when, while maintaining their unique individuality, they enter the great community and thus prepare themselves to be divine creators, just as they were with creator gods before they walked on the earth as human beings.

Human evolution began with divine being and will return to it. The diverse human I-beings will be individual but at the same time united in a community, in a unity that will give birth to a new planetary body called 'The New Jerusalem' in the Apocalypse. The human self will be born into I-being and then the harmony of the spheres will echo the words of the Mystery of Golgotha: 'My God, my God, how you have glorified me!' [. . .]

Extract from a lecture given in Berlin on 25 March 1907

[. . .] Regard this not as a picture but as a reality. Regard the amount of blood that flowed from Christ's wounds as the amount that had to flow so that blood would lose the tendency to establish narrow communities and thus acquire the potential to spread community over the entire earth.

Perhaps no one has come as close to touching on this mystery exoterically as Richard Wagner in his essay about his opera *Parsifal.* Here he touches on the deepest truths of the mysteries. If you look at it in this way you will see that the meaning of Christianity lies in dissolving all that is bound to tribes, families and narrowly delimited communities on the one hand, and on the other in making human beings into separate, unique entities so that they experience themselves both as individuals and members of humanity as a whole. [. . .]

The effects began with Whitsun, when the Holy Spirit was poured out. When people learn to speak out of the souls of others they will no longer speak egotistically. This can best be presented in the picture of the disciples speaking to all peoples in all tongues. Hence the Holy Spirit prepared what is to be achieved through the blood of the Son, the Logos, the Christ. [. . .]

11. Transforming Sexuality

Extract from a lecture given in Berlin on 19 May 1905

In this passage Steiner focuses on the pivotal dynamic between the magician Klingsor's 'Chastel Merveille' or castle of wonders, and the Grail castle of Mont Salvat, highlighting the different attitudes to sexuality that these embody. By merely 'destroying the organ of desire'—partly at least perhaps a metaphor for extreme practices of Christian asceticism—without working through and transforming desire itself, Klingsor gains a suppressive ascendancy over the flesh without any possibility of higher development. Such aggressive asceticism stands in stark contrast to Parzival's developing compassion for all life, for instance as embodied in the animal kingdom. It is not a matter of denying sensory nature but of acknowledging, loving and slowly enhancing and transforming it.

Let us briefly recall the tale of 'Poor Henry':[19] a Swabian knight who has always been fortunate in life is suddenly struck by an incurable disease which can only be healed by the sacrifice and death of a pure virgin. A virgin is found who is willing to sacrifice herself. They go to Salerno, to a famous physician. At the last moment however, Henry regrets the sacrifice and decides not to accept it. The virgin does not die, Henry regains his health after all, and the two marry.

Here we have, therefore, a pure virgin and her sacrifice on behalf of a man who has only lived a life of pleasure and who is saved through her sacrifice. A mystery lies concealed in this. From the standpoint of the Middle Ages, in the 'Minnesänger' tradition,[20] [...] love based on the life of the senses was considered as something that had been overcome;

love was to rise again spiritually, linked with the feeling of renunciation.

To realize what took place here we must compile all the aspects which can recreate for us the countenance or physiognomy of that past period. And then we will be able to understand what inspired Wagner in presenting this legend of Parzival.

The earliest Teutonic races had a legend we can trace throughout history—one of the ancient legends that can also be found in Italy and other countries in somewhat different form. Let us recall this legend in outline: a man has learned to know the pleasures and joys of this world and penetrates into a kind of subterranean cavern. There he meets a woman of great charm and allure. He experiences paradisiacal joys—but nevertheless longs to return to the earth. This legend surfaces throughout Europe and it comes clearly to the fore in Tannhäuser. If we study this legend we will find that it is, to begin with, a depiction and embodiment of love in Germanic countries before the time of Christ. Life in the external world is renounced in favour of withdrawing into the cavern, to the joys of the old kind of love which the goddess Venus provides.

In this form this legend has no opportunity to look up to something higher, and it arose before views of love underwent the transformation we mentioned. Later, in the early Christian period, people sought to draw a stark contrast between this earlier period, this paradise in the cave of Venus, and the other, spiritual paradise they found. [...]

We must consider once more what it means that 'Poor Henry' is healed by a pure virgin. Henry has to begin with lived a life of the senses, and his sense of self is sustained by racial connections. This self begins to ail as soon as it starts to hear the higher call, which invokes a sense for the whole of humanity. The soul grows ill because it connects itself with something which is rooted only in the race: with a form of love rooted in the tribe or race. Now this lower kind of love living in the race must be redeemed by something higher, by the higher, purer soul that is ready to sacrifice itself for the striving human soul.

You know that the soul consists of a male and female aspect, and that the sensory impressions which enter the soul push its feminine aspect into the background. Goethe's phrase in part 2 of *Faust,* 'The eternal feminine draws us upwards and on', shows how sense life is overcome, a salvation and redemption we also find in *Tristan and Isolde.*

The overcoming of sensory life is embodied historically in the name and figure of Parzival, the representative of a new kind of Christianity. He becomes the king of the Holy Grail because he redeems what has once been held in bondage by the senses and thus brings a new principle of love into the world. What is Parzival based on? What is the meaning of the Holy Grail? The earliest legend which appears at the turning point of the Middle Ages tells us that the Holy Grail is the cup used by Christ Jesus at the Last Supper, the cup in which He offered the bread and the wine and in which Joseph of Arimathea caught the blood streaming from Christ's wound. The spear which caused this wound, and the chalice, were carried up by angels who bore them aloft in the air. Titurel found them, and built upon Mont Salvat a castle in which he could guard these treasures. Twelve knights gathered together to serve the Holy Grail, which had the power to avert the danger of death from these knights and to supply them with everything they needed for their life. Whenever they looked upon the Grail they acquired new spiritual strength.

On the one hand we have the temple of the Holy Grail with its knights, and on the other the magic castle of Klingsor with his own knights, the enemies of the knighthood of the Grail. Here we meet two forms of Christianity. Klingsor has mutilated himself so as not to fall prey to the senses. Yet he has not overcome his desires, merely depriving himself of the possibility of satisfying them. Thus he still lives in a sensual sphere. The maidens of the magic castle serve him, and everything belonging to the sphere of desires is at his disposal. Kundry is the real temptress in this kingdom;[21] she attracts everyone who approaches Klingsor into the sphere of sensual love. Klingsor has not destroyed desire but only the organ of desire, and thus personifies the form of Christianity which came from the south and introduced the life of asceticism. It eliminated sensual life but it could not destroy desire, nor protect against the tempting powers of Kundry. A higher element was perceived in the power of spirituality which rises above sensual life into the sphere of purified love; not through compulsion or suppression, but through higher, spiritual knowledge.

Amfortas and the knights of the Holy Grail strive for this higher life, but do not succeed in establishing its kingdom. So long as true spiritual power is lacking, Amfortas yields to the temptations of Kundry. The higher spirituality personified in Amfortas falls prey to the lower memory.

Thus we can see two phenomena: on the one hand a Christianity which has embraced asceticism but is unable to attain higher spiritual knowledge; and on the other the spiritual knighthood which falls prey to Klingsor's temptation until the appearance of the one who vanquishes Klingsor and brings about redemption. Amfortas is wounded and loses the secret spear, and must guard the Grail as a flawed and sorrow-laden king. This higher Christianity is therefore diseased and in pain. It must guard the Christian mysteries until a new saviour appears in the figure of Parzival.

Parzival must first learn his lesson, and pass through trials. Becoming purified he finally attains to spiritual power, a sense of the great unity of all being. Richard Wagner has thus intuitively come to great esoteric truths—firstly to compassion. Parzival passes through a range of experiences which fill him with compassion for our older brothers, the animals. In his fierce desire to embrace knighthood he has abandoned his mother Herzeleide, who has died of a broken heart. He has fought battles and killed; but then the dying glance of an animal teaches him what it really means to kill.

The second stage involves rising above desire, without killing or suppressing it from without.

Thus he reaches the sanctuary of the Grail, without as yet understanding his task. Life teaches him. He is tempted by Kundry but stands the test. At the point of succumbing, he rises above desire as a new, pure love shines forth within him like a rising sun. Something flares up in him which we already discovered in the *Twilight of the Gods: 'Incarnatus est de spiritu sancto ex Maria Virgine'*—'Born of the spirit through the virgin' (who embodies the higher love not pervaded by sensual feelings).

The human being must awaken within him a soul which purifies everything transmitted by the senses, because virgin substance, virgin matter, will give birth to the Christ I. The lower feminine element in the human soul dies and will be replaced by a higher feminine element which raises us to the spirit. A higher, virgin power opposes the seductress Kundry. Kundry, the other feminine aspect which seeks to draw human beings down into sex alone, must be overcome. [...] Emancipation from a love dependent on the senses—this is the mystery which Wagner has woven into his *Parsifal.*

12. The Higher Calyx

Extract from a lecture given in Nuremberg on 2 December 1907

Together, the plant, animal and human kingdoms can be seen as a kind of cross. The plant rises from the earth and offers its calyx to the sun to effect a kind of reproduction that is chaste, without the inner turbulence of passions and desires. The word 'calyx' of course is almost synonymous with 'chalice' and thus suggests a Grail quality. The human being, in contrast, has his 'roots' (the brain and nervous system) in the air and a reproductive system that is earth-oriented. Thus we can see ourselves, in a certain sense, as reversed plants. The animal, as the horizontal arm of the cross, develops desires but is still much more in tune than we are with the natural rhythms of the earth. In raising ourselves out of the natural world in the course of evolution we have, at the same time, immersed our soul nature ever deeper in matter. The cross at Golgotha embodies the point at which this deepening descent is reversed and we can start the slow ascent towards a form of humanity that, at a new, higher and conscious level, recovers the selfless purity of the flower, as a kind of independent yet inter-dependent existence in spiritual community.

[...] We must always turn to legends for enlightenment about significant turning-points in evolution, for the truths they contain are deeper than those recorded in history. Legends show us how the forces and influences of initiates intervene in the course of history and should not be regarded as accounts of external events.

The period of transition from universal clairvoyant consciousness to individualized ego consciousness was of the greatest significance, and we find it expressed in the Lohengrin myth. This is an age when the new spirit emerges from the old. Two zeitgeists confront one another. Elsa, the feminine principle, represents the soul striving for the highest spirit. Conventional interpretations of Goethe's words in the 'Chorus Mysticus' at the end of his *Faust* are terribly banal, whereas in reality they derive from the very depths of mysticism: 'The eternal feminine leads us upwards and on.' The human soul must be quickened by the mighty events through which new principles find their way into evolution. [. . .]

Now there is a certain profound mystery bound up with humanity and it is depicted symbolically in a myth. When at the beginning of our evolution Lucifer fell from the ranks of spirits who guide humanity, a precious stone fell from his crown. This stone was the cup from which Christ Jesus drank with His disciples at the Last Supper and in which the blood flowing on Golgotha was received. The cup passed to Joseph of Arimathea who brought it to the West. After many wanderings it came into the hands of Titurel who founded the citadel of the Grail. The cup was guarded by the 'holy love-lance', and the legend says that all who looked upon the Grail acquired something of an immortal quality.

And now let us think of the mystery contained in this myth as a metaphor for human evolution, as indeed it is known to be by those who understand the mysteries of the Grail. In the earlier phases of evolution on earth, all love was bound up with the blood. Blood relationship dictated human community. Marriage took place between those who were united by a blood tie. The point at which marriage ceased to be only between those of the same kith and kin marked an important transition. Consciousness of this truth is expressed in many sagas and myths. To begin with, as we have said, love was bound up with blood kinship, and later on the circle within which human beings joined in marriage grew ever wider. This was the one stream in evolution: love dependent on ties of flesh and blood.

But later on, a different principle began to hold sway—that of individual independence. [. . .] The words of Christ are to be interpreted thus: he who forsakes not father and mother—that is to say, he who cannot substitute for a love that is bound up with flesh and blood, a love that flows from soul to soul, from brother to sister, from one human being to all human beings—he 'cannot be my disciple'.

A stone falls from Lucifer's crown and this stone becomes the holy cup wherein the Christ principle is united with the Lucifer-principle of independence. Knowledge of this mighty impulse developed the power of the I or ego in the knights of the Grail. And to those who were pupils in the mysteries of the Holy Grail the following teaching was given. (I am summarizing in a single passage what pupils of the Grail were shown in gradual stages [. . .].)

> *Look at the plant. Do not compare its flower with the human head. The flower, with its male and female organs of fertilization, in fact corresponds to the human sexual system. The root of the plant is what actually corresponds to the human head. [. . .] The human being is a plant reversed. He has accomplished a complete reversal. In chastity and purity the plant stretches out its calyx towards the light, receiving its rays, receiving the 'holy love-lance', the 'kiss' which ripens the fruit. The animal has turned only half-way. The plant, whose 'head' penetrates into the earth, the animal with its spine in a horizontal direction, and the human being with his*

> *upright posture and his upward gaze—together these form the shape of the cross. [. . .] Plato spoke truly when he said that the soul of the cosmos lies crucified in the body of the world. The cosmic soul, pervading plant, animal and human being, lives in bodies which, together, represent the cross.*

In what sense have we human beings accomplished this complete reversal of the plant? According to the true insights of mysticism, plant consciousness is that of a person asleep. When asleep, we are in a sense like a plant. We acquired the consciousness that is ours today by permeating the pure plant body with desires, with the body of passions. By doing so we progressed on the path to self-awareness. But this has been achieved at the cost of permeating pure plant-substance with desire.

The pupils of the Grail were told of a state to which human beings would attain in future. Possessed of clear, alert consciousness, their being would be purified, the substance of the human body would become as pure and chaste as that of the plant, and their organs of reproduction transformed. The idea living in the minds of the knights of the Grail was that the human being of the future will have powers of reproduction not filled with the element of desire but as chaste and pure as the calyx which turns towards the 'love-lance'—the rays of the sun. The Grail ideal will be fulfilled when the human being brings forth his like with the purity and chastity of the plant, when he brings forth his own image in the higher calyx and becomes a creator in the spirit. This ideal was known as the Holy Grail: the transformed reproductive organs which bring forth the human being as purely and as chastely as the word is brought forth today by the waves of air working through the larynx.

And now let us see how this sublime ideal lived in the heart and soul of Richard Wagner. On Good Friday 1857, he was standing on the balcony of the summer house at Wesendonck Villa; as he looked out over the landscape he saw the budding of early spring flowers. The sight of the young plants revealed to him the mystery of the Holy Grail, the mystery of birth of all that is implicit in the image of the Holy Grail. All this he felt in connection with Good Friday, and in the mood that arose in him the first idea for *Parsifal* was born. Many things happened in the intervening period but the feeling remained in him and out of it he created the figure of Parsifal—the figure in whom knowledge is sublimated to feeling; who, having suffered for others, acquires 'compassionate knowledge'. And the Amfortas mystery shows how human nature in the course of evolution has been wounded by the lance of defiled love.

Such, then, is the mystery of the Holy Grail. It must be approached with the greatest delicacy; we should try to engage with its whole mood and feeling and let the ideas in their entirety resonate in our souls. [. . .]

13. The Resonant Chalice

Extract from a lecture given in Stuttgart on
16 September 1907

The images reproduced here evoke, symbolize and sum up many of the themes so far addressed in this section and give a grand overview of human evolution into the distant future, to stages of humanity that at present seem very far-off and hard to conceive of. The larynx will, says Steiner, unite more closely with the heart and become a chalice that both resonates with and co-creates spiritual realities. Though this may strike some as far-fetched, sound vibrations have been shown to exert a formative effect on matter—for instance in the so-called 'Chladni' plates where a violin bow configures sand into beautiful geometric patterns. We know how the sound of a beautiful voice, in speech or song, can transport us and vibrate through us, and it is perhaps not such a huge imaginative leap to consider that this might one day extend to actually engendering life. In the ancient Finnish epic Kalevala, the dead hero Lemminkainen, whose limbs have been torn asunder, is brought back to life by the singing and spells of his mother: just one image among many in world culture for the potency of the voice.

In the seven seals that were hung in the festival hall during the Munich Congress of 1907, we have a picture of human evolution side by side with that of the world to which we belong. Let us see what they show us.

The first seal shows a person clad in white, his feet of molten metal, and a fiery sword projecting from the mouth. His right hand is surrounded by the signs of our planets—

First seal

Saturn, Sun, Moon, Mars, Mercury, Jupiter, Venus. Those familiar with the Apocalypse of St John will remember that it contains a description that closely corresponds to this picture, for St John was an initiate. This seal, one can say, represents the idea of humanity as a whole. [. . .] When we go back in human evolution, we come to a time when human beings were at an imperfect stage. Thus, for example, they did not have heads resembling those you carry on your shoulders today. It would sound grotesque, indeed, if I described the people of those times to you. Only gradually did the head develop; and it will continue developing. Human beings also have organs today that have completed their evolution and in the future they will no longer form part of the human body. There are others that will be transformed. An example is the larynx which, certainly, has an important future connection with the heart. At present the larynx is still only at the beginning of its development, but in times to come it will be transformed into a spiritualized organ of reproduction. You can get some idea of this mystery if you reflect on what we can do with our larynx today.

While I speak to you, you hear my words. By virtue of the fact that this sound fills the air and that certain vibrations are produced in it, my words are conveyed to your ears and to your souls. When I say a word, for example 'world', the air vibrates in an embodiment of that word. What we produce in this way today can be called 'creating in the mineral kingdom'. The movements of the air are mineral movements, so to speak, and thus through the larynx we have a mineral effect on our environment. But human beings will progress and evolve and will also come to exert an effect in the plant realm. They will then call forth not only mineral, but also plant-like vibrations. They will speak 'plants' into being. The next step will be a developing human capacity to speak 'feeling entities' into being. At the highest stage of their development, they will generate their like through the larynx, will reproduce themselves. Today a person can only express the contents of his soul through his larynx, but then he will literally 'express' his own kind. As people in the future will be able to call people into being through their speech, so the forerunners of mankind, the gods, were gifted with an organ with which they expressed and gave life to all things that surround us today. It is they who made manifest all the animals and everything else. In the literal sense of the word, all of you are words uttered by divine beings.

'In the beginning was the Word, and the Word was with God, and a God was the Word!' This does not mean a philosophical word in the speculative sense; St John set down a primal fact that is to be taken quite literally.

At the end the Word will still be. Creation is a realization of the Word, and in the future human beings will bring forth living realizations of what today they express in speech. At that stage people will no longer have the physical forms they have today; they will have progressed to the form that existed on Saturn, to fire matter.

The being who spoke forth all that exists in the world today is the great prototype of human beings. His utterance created Saturn in the universe, the Sun, Moon, Earth, Mercury, Jupiter and Venus. The seven planets in the seal point to this. They are the sign that indicates the height to which a human being will eventually be able to evolve. Our planet then will consist of fiery matter, and we will be able to speak creatively into this fiery matter. The fiery sword that projects from the mouth of the figure in the seal represents this. All will be fiery, hence the feet of flowing metal. [. . .]

The next picture shows us that when he achieves the highest spirituality the human being takes on the form of Michael fettering evil in the world, symbolized by the dragon.

In a certain way we have seen that both at the beginning and at the end of human evolution the same conditions and transformations hold sway. We have seen them portrayed in the figure with the feet of molten fire and the sword projecting from his mouth. In symbolism of great profundity, the world's whole being is now revealed to us in the symbol of the Holy Grail.

Sixth seal

Let me set this seal before your eyes in a few words. The occultist knows that space in the physical world is not simply void but something quite different. Space is the source from which all beings have, so to speak, physically crystallized. Imagine a cube-shaped, transparent glass vessel filled with water. Now imagine that certain cooling streams are led through this water so that it congeals in the most manifold forms into ice. This will give you an idea of the world's creation, of space, and of the divine creative word spoken into it. The occultist presents this space into which the divine creative Word has been spoken as the transparent cube. Within this space various beings develop. The ones standing nearest to us can be characterized as follows. The cube has three perpendicular directions, three axes, length, height and breadth. It thus represents the three dimensions in space. Now imagine the counter-dimensions to these three outside dimensions of the physical world. You may visualize this by imagining someone moving in one direction and colliding with someone else coming from another direction. Similarly, there is a counter-dimension to every dimension of space, so that in all we have six counter-rays. These counter-rays represent the primal beginnings of the highest human members. The physical body, crystallized from space, is the lowest. The spiritual, the highest, is the opposite counter-dimension. In their development, these counter-dimensions first form themselves in an entity best described when we let them flow together into the world of passions, sensual appetites and instincts. This it is at first. Later, it becomes something else. It becomes ever more purified—we have seen to what height—but it issued from the lower impulses, which are here symbolized by the snake. The process of purification is symbolized by the counter-dimensions converging in two snakes standing opposite each other. As mankind purifies itself, it rises through what is called the world spiral. The purified body of the snake, this world spiral, has deep significance. [...]

[...] You see here how the spiral has significance for celestial bodies, and these describe a form with which human beings will one day identify. At that time, a person's generative power will be cleansed and purified, and his larynx will become his generative organ. The purified snake body we will have developed will no longer work upwards from below, but from above downwards. The transformed larynx

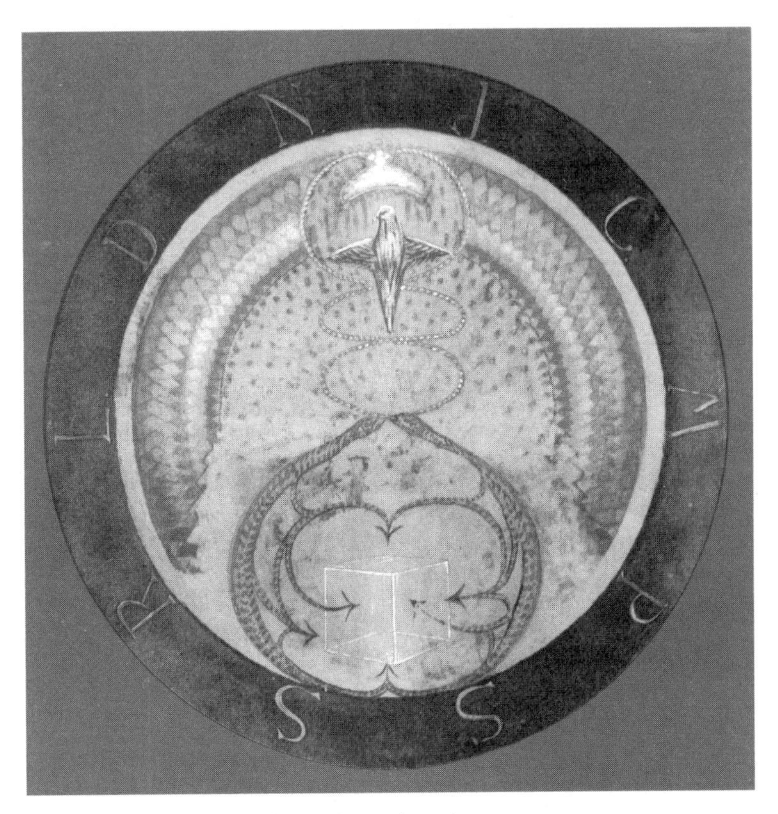

Seventh seal

will become the chalice known as the Holy Grail. As one is purified, so cosmic essence and energy will unite with this generative organ. This cosmic spirit in its essence is represented by the dove facing the Holy Grail. Here it symbolizes the spiritualized fertilization received from the cosmos when human beings have identified with it. The all-embracing creativity of this process is represented by the rainbow. This is the seal of the Holy Grail. The whole gives a wonderful sense of the connection between cosmos and human beings, as a summation of the meaning of the other seals.

14. Seeing I to I

Extract from a lecture given in Berlin on 6 January 1906

In this passage, the social aspect of the Grail comes to the fore, and is related closely with the future mastery of life forces. At present we can only control physical forces in the mineral, material world, creating buildings and technologies that express human endeavour and striving. We will not achieve the stage of consciously mastering and creating life, says Steiner, until we also attain a higher, harmonious, all-embracing community. Logical and intellectual agreement about indisputable truths—such as mathematical truths—can today give us an inkling of how in future we might achieve unanimity in all other realms of human experience, founded on all-encompassing love. Such community cannot be imposed but must arise freely in the soul of each separate individual, as it does, slowly, during Parzival's trials. While these are far-off goals, such ideas also have immediate relevance in modern societies, with all their conflicts, classes and divisions. What unifies us above and beyond—and without suppressing—differences, in a way that allows every individual to weave his particular and distinct gifts into the social fabric? According to Steiner, the only way to do this is by each of us individually developing spiritual perception and learning to resonate truly with the laws at work in the cosmos. The healing and transforming of the division between the sexes is one level where this work can start.

The symbol of all that we do nothing to achieve, of what is simply given us, is drawn from sexual life. There the human being is, indeed, productive, but what manifests in this productive power has nothing to do with human art, science or ability. From it is excluded everything which comes to expression in the three pillars[22] of the 'royal art'. So when some present these sexual symbols to humanity they mean: in this symbol is expressed human nature not as we ourselves have made it, but as it was given us by the gods. This finds its expression in Abel, the hunter and herdsman, who offers the sacrificial animal, the lamb, thus offering what he himself has done nothing to produce and which came into existence without his help.

What did Cain offer, in contrast? He sacrificed what he obtained by his own labour, what he had won from the fruits of the earth by tilling the soil. What he sacrificed needed human skill, knowledge and wisdom; it required comprehension of what one has done, based, in a spiritual sense, on human freedom to decide things for ourselves. This has to be paid for with guilt: by killing first of all the living things nature gives, which divine powers give, just as Cain slew Abel.

Through guilt lies the path to freedom. Everything which divine powers endow us with and which we can at best act on only in a secondary way, is given us primarily in the kingdoms of nature over which we have no control. These kingdoms (the plant, animal and human) are not available for any primary human contribution because they are perpetuated by physical reproduction. All the reproductive forces in these kingdoms are granted us by nature. Insofar as we take what is living for our use—because the world is our dwelling place, evolved from living things—we offer the sacrifice only of what is simply given to us, as Abel offered the sacrifice given to him.

The symbol of these three kingdoms is the cross. The lower beam symbolizes the plant kingdom, the middle or cross beam the animal kingdom, and the upper beam the human kingdom.

The plant has its roots buried in the earth and directs upwards, in the blossom, those parts which in us are directed downwards. In the blossom appear the plant's reproductive organs. The downwards directed part of the plant, the root, is the plant's head, buried in the earth. The animal is the plant turned half way, carrying its backbone in a horizontal orientation in relation to the earth. The human being is the plant turned completely around, so that the lower part corresponding to the root, the head, is directed upwards.

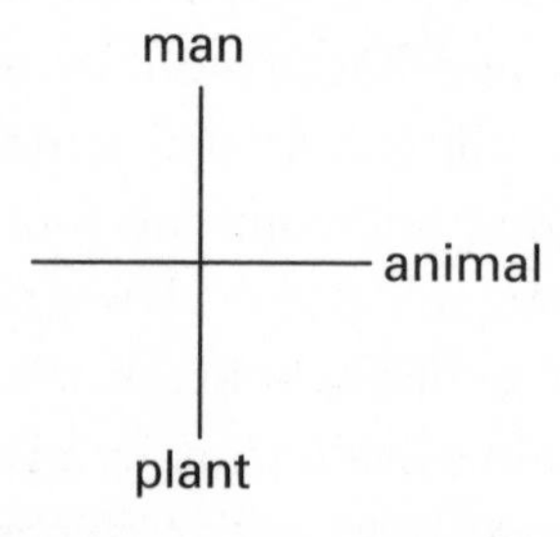

This underlies all the mysteries relating to the cross. Theosophy shows us how the human being must pass in the course of his evolution through the various kingdoms of nature, through the plant, animal and human kingdoms. This is the same thing as Plato expressed in the beautiful words: 'The world soul is nailed to the cross of the world body.' The human soul is a spark struck from the world soul, and the human being, as physical human being, is plant, animal and physical human being at the same time. Insofar as the world soul has divided itself into the individual sparks of human souls it is, as it were, nailed to what is expressed in the three kingdoms of plant, animal and human. Powers we have not mastered are at work in these kingdoms. If we wish to master them we must create a new kingdom of our own, which is not expressed in the cross.

When talking of this subject I am often asked: Where is the mineral kingdom in all this? The mineral kingdom is not symbolized in the cross because it is there that human beings can already express themselves in blindingly clear ways, where we have learned to apply the techniques of weighing and calculating, or geometry and arithmetic; in fact, everything pertaining to inorganic nature, to the mineral kingdom.

If you contemplate a temple you can see that the human being has erected it with ruler, compass, square, plumb line and spirit level, and finally with the thinking that inorganic nature has transmitted to the architect in geometry and mechanics. And as you continue your contemplation of the whole temple you will find it to be an inanimate object born out of human freedom and brainwork. You cannot say this, however, if you observe a plant or an animal.

So you see that what human beings have mastered, what we can master, has so far been the inanimate realm. And everything which the human being has converted to harmony and order out of the inanimate world is the symbol of his 'royal art' on earth. If you go back to the time of the ancient Chaldeans and Egyptians—when not only the intellect was used in building but when heightened perceptions permeated everything, the mastery of inorganic nature was then seen as the royal art—which is why control of nature was characterized as 'free masonry'. [...]

Look back to the construction of the Egyptian pyramids, in which stone was fitted to stone through human agency. Nature's creation was given a new form as a result of human thought. Human wisdom has thus transformed the earth. [...] This is the first pillar, that of wisdom.

Somewhat later we see the second pillar established, the

pillar of beauty, of art. Art is likewise a means to pour the human spirit into lifeless matter, and again the result is an ensoulment of the inanimate in nature. Try for a moment to picture in your mind how the wisdom in art gradually overcomes and masters lifeless nature, and you will see how what is initially there without our participation is reshaped by us. One can visualize how the whole earth has been transformed by human hands, how the whole earth has become a work of art, full of wisdom and radiating beauty: built by human hands, radiating human wisdom. This may seem fantastic, but is more than that. It is in fact humanity's mission on earth to transform the planet artistically. You find this expressed in the second pillar, that of beauty.

To this you can add, as the third pillar, the reshaping of the human race in the life of nations and states: the propagation of the human spirit in the world, in the lifeless realm. [. . .] Even the statesman or politician structures what is naturally endowed. [. . .]

Thus the medieval thinker of the twelfth century looked back at the esoteric wisdom of the ancient Chaldeans, at Greek art and beauty and at the strength embodied in the Roman state. These are the three great pillars of world history—wisdom, beauty and strength. Goethe portrayed them in his 'fairy-tale' as the three kings: esoteric wisdom in the Gold King, beauty as in Greece in the Silver King, and, in the Brass King, strength as embodied in the Roman concept of the state and then adopted in the organization of the Christian Church. And the Middle Ages, with its chaos, resulting from the effect of migrating peoples, and with its mixtures of styles, is expressed in the misshapen Mixed King made of gold, silver and brass. In him, what was separate in various ancient cultures, is all mixed together. Later these separate forces will once again need to develop and emerge from this chaotic mix to a higher level.

All who took the Holy Grail as their symbol in the Middle Ages set themselves the task of using human powers to bring these separate forces to a higher stage of development. The Holy Grail was to be something essentially new, even though its symbolism is closely related to the symbols of a very ancient mystical tradition.

What then is the Holy Grail? For those who can properly understand this legend it signifies the following:

Until now, the human being has only mastered the inanimate forces of nature. Transformation of the living forces, of what sprouts and grows in the plants, and of what manifests in animal [and human] reproduction, is beyond his power. Human beings as yet have no access to these mysterious powers of nature and cannot encroach on them. They cannot fully comprehend what results from these forces. [. . .] But just as human beings have gained mastery of inanimate nature and gravitational forces with spirit level and plumb line, with geometry and mechanics, so in future they will come to control what at present they receive only as a gift from nature or from divine powers—that is, living forces. [. . .]

In the Middle Ages a radically new impetus was thus introduced into Freemasonry, and is denoted by the symbol of the Holy Grail, as the power of self-sacrifice. I have often said that harmony in human relationships is not brought about by preaching it but by creating it. Once the necessary forces have been awoken in human nature, lack of brotherliness can no longer persist. Such concepts as 'majority' and 'minority' become meaningless. [. . .]

Although our age is not yet so advanced as to be able to master living forces, and although the era has not yet arrived when living and life-giving forces can be consciously employed, a preparatory school for this endeavour already exists, founded by the movement called the Lodge of the Holy Grail. The time will come however—a quite specific point in time—when humanity, unlike now, will recognize that deep, inward soul forces cannot be decided by majority decisions; that no vote can settle questions involving the limitless realm of love, or what one feels or senses. The force common to all humanity, which comes to expression in the mind as an all-embracing unity about which there can be no conflict, is called manas. And when human beings have reached the stage of being not only one in their intellect but also in their perceptions and feelings, and are in harmony in their inmost souls—meeting one another in what is noble and good, lovingly joining in one objective in the same way that nowadays they agree that two times two makes four, and three times three equals nine—then the time will also have arrived when they can master living forces too. Unanimity—objective unanimity of perception and feeling—with a love encompassing all humanity, is the precondition for achieving mastery over the forces of life.

Those who founded the movement of the Holy Grail in the twelfth century said that this control over living nature was at one time available to the gods who created the cosmos and descended to earth to give humanity the germ of the capacity for the same divine forces they themselves already possessed. Thus the human being is now on the way to becoming a god, having something in his inner being which strives upwards towards where the gods once stood. Today, the intellect [manas] is the predominant force; in the future it will be love [buddhi] and, in a still more distant future, human beings will attain the stage of atma.

Combined, these powers give humanity mastery over what is symbolized by the cross. The gods' use of this power is embodied in the symbol of a triangle with its apex pointing downwards.

Divine power

Expressed through human beings, striving from below upwards towards the divine, this force is symbolized by a triangle with apex pointing upwards.

Human strength

The gods have raised themselves out of human nature and withdrawn; but they have left behind the triangle which will develop further in us. This triangle is also the symbol of the Holy Grail.

The symbol of the Holy Grail

The medieval occultist expressed the symbol of the Grail—the symbol for awakening perfection in the living realm—in the form of a triangle. This does not necessitate a common Church encircling the globe with rigid organizational forms, although this may well give something to the individual soul. But if all souls are to strike the same note then the power of the Holy Grail must be awoken in each individual. Whoever wants to awaken the power of the Grail within him will gain nothing by asking the powers of the official Church to kindly instruct him. Instead he must awaken this power in himself, without asking others' permission too much. We start from dullness and progress through doubt to strength. This pilgrimage of the soul is expressed in the figure of Parzival who seeks the Holy Grail. This is one of the many diverse deeper meanings of the Parzival figure.

Does it further my knowledge if a corporate body, however wise and great, issues an official proclamation of the truth? If I want to learn mathematics I must study it and gain an understanding of it for myself. And what use is it if such a corporate body possesses the power of the cross? If I wish to make use of this power, mastery of the living realm, I must achieve this myself. No one else can tell it to me or communicate it through words: at best they can show it to me in the symbol, give me the shining symbol of the Grail, but it cannot be told in an intellectual formula.

The first achievement of this medieval occultism, therefore, was what appeared in so many different movements in Europe: the striving for individual religious experience, and escape from the rigid uniformity of the organized Church. You can scarcely grasp the extent to which this tendency underlies Wolfram von Eschenbach's *Parzival*. What manifested for the first time during the Reformation was already inherent in the Grail symbol. Those who have a sense of the profound meaning symbols can embody will understand this symbol's deep cultural significance. The great things of the world are not born in noise and tumult but in intimacy and stillness. Humanity's development does not advance by the thunder of cannons but through the strength of what is born in the intimacy of such secret brotherhoods, and of what is expressed in such world-encompassing symbols which inspire humanity.

Since that time, through innumerable channels, human hearts have received an influx from what was conceived by those initiated into the mysteries of the Holy Grail in the middle of the twelfth century. Such individuals had to hide from the world and live anonymously. But really they were the leaven preparing the culture of the past 400 years. [. . .]

Slowly but surely, humanity's development will come to embrace organic, living forces. A time will come—however fantastic this may seem now—when people will no longer paint only pictures, will no longer make only lifeless sculptures, but will be able to breathe life into what they now merely paint, merely form with colour or with a chisel.

What may appear less fantastic is that this is already dawning in a particular sphere: these living forces are already starting to intervene in the life of society. That is the real secret surrounding the Grail. The last event initiated in the social sphere by old Freemasonry was the French Revolution. Here the basic ideas of Freemasonry came out into the open as 'equality, liberty and fraternity'. Those who know this are also aware that ideas emanating from the Grail were propagated through innumerable channels and constituted the really active force in the French Revolution.

The socialism of today exists only as an abortive and impossible experiment: as a final, desperate struggle, one can say, in a receding wave of humanity's evolution. It cannot achieve any really positive result. What it tries to achieve can only be achieved through living activity; the pillar of strength is not enough. Socialism can no longer be controlled through inanimate forces. The ideas of the French Revolution—liberty, equality, fraternity—were the last ideas to flow out of the inanimate. Everything that still runs on that track is fruitless and doomed to die. The great evil existing in the world today, the dire misery that comes to expression with such terrible power in what is called the 'social question', can no longer be controlled by inanimate means. A royal art is needed for that; and this was inaugurated in the symbol of the Holy Grail.

Through this royal art human beings must come to control something similar to what sprouts in the plant—the same force that the occultist uses when he accelerates the growth of a plant before him. In a similar way, something of this force must be used for social salvation. This power, which is described by those who know something of the Rosicrucian mysteries—as, for example, Bulwer Lytton did in his futuristic novel *The Coming Race*[23]—is at present still at an elementary, germinal stage. In the Freemasonry of the future, it will become the real content of the higher degrees. The royal art will, in the future, be a social art. [...]

What the human spirit has given shape to, in matter, will remain present in the world as a continuing force. Cologne's Gothic cathedral will for example pass away; but it is of far-reaching significance that the atoms were once in this form. This form itself is the imperishable thing that will henceforth participate in humanity's ongoing process of evolution, just as the plant's living force participates in nature's evolution! The painter who paints a picture today, who imprints dead matter with his own intensity of soul, is also creating something that will sooner or later be dispersed in thousands of atoms. What is imperishable and has lasting value, what is eternal, is that he has *created*, that something has flowed into matter from his soul.

States and all other human communities come and go before our eyes. But these communities formed by human souls constitute humanly-conceived ideas of eternal value, with eternally enduring significance. And when this human race once again appears on earth in a new form, then it will see the fruits of these elements of eternal value.

Whoever turns his gaze upwards to the starry heavens today sees a wonderful harmony which has evolved—it was not always there. When we build a cathedral we place stone upon stone; when we paint a picture we place colour next to colour; when we organize a community we make law upon law. In exactly the same way, creative beings once worked upon and fashioned what we see today before us in the cosmos. Neither moon nor sun would shine, no plant would reproduce, unless everything we find in the cosmos had not once been fashioned by beings who worked as we work today on refashioning the cosmos. Just as we work upon the cosmos today through wisdom, beauty and strength, so too did beings who do not belong to our present human kingdom once work on the cosmos.

Any harmony is always the outcome of a former disharmony. Just as stones abounded in a perplexing variety of forms before they were given form as a Greek temple, thus becoming a coordinated structure, and just as the profusion of colours on a palette is meaningfully arrayed in a picture, so all matter was in other chaotic relationships before the creative spirit transformed it into this cosmos. The same thing is being recapitulated at a new level, and only he who sees the whole can properly work on the details. Everything of real significance for humanity's progress has been brought about with care and judgement, through initiation into the great laws at work in the world. What the day produces is ephemeral. What is created in the day through knowledge of the eternal laws is, however, imperishable. Freemasonry really means creating in the day with knowledge of eternal laws.

In fact one can say that, properly understood, Freemasonry engenders all art, science and religion, all that goes beyond what the gods give us as expressed in the symbol of the cross. In this sense Freemasonry is intimately involved in everything that human hands have shaped. Everything that culture has created from raw, inanimate matter. [. . .]

In the end, everything must undergo schooling. The last 400 years were a schooling for humanity—the school of godlessness, purely human experimentation: from a certain perspective a return to chaos. Everyone is experimenting today, without being aware of our connection with higher worlds—apart from those who have once more sought and found that connection. Nearly everyone lives entirely for himself today, without perceiving anything of the real, all-penetrating common design. And this of course is also what causes such terrible dissatisfaction everywhere.

What we need is a renewal of the Grail chivalry in a modern form. By approaching this we can come to know the real forces still lying concealed within human evolution.

Today so many people take up the old symbols without understanding them; what is thus, uncomprehendingly, made of sexual symbols comes nowhere near a correct understanding of Masonic concepts. Such understanding is to be sought in precisely those things which redeem natural forces: in penetrating and mastering what is living in the same way that the geometrician penetrates and masters inanimate matter with his rule, compasses, spirit level and so forth; and in working upon the living in the same way that those who build a temple place stones together. [. . .]

There is a very ancient symbol in Freemasonry, the so-called Tau. This is basically nothing other than a cross from which an arm has been removed. If one lets the plant kingdom come into play, one obtains the upwards-directed cross [. . .]:

You may remember the legend of Hiram Abiff I spoke of in my last lecture on Freemasonry; of how, at a particular moment he makes use of the Tau sign when the Queen of Sheba wishes him to summon all the workers engaged in building the temple. The people working together in social partnership would never appear at Solomon's command; but at the sign of the Tau, which Hiram Abiff raises aloft, they appear from all sides. The Tau symbolizes an entirely new power, based on freedom and involving the awakening of a new natural force. [. . .]

One can easily understand that control over inanimate nature leads to such things as wireless telegraphy, working across a great distance from the transmitter to the receiving station. The apparatus can be set to work at will, is effective over great distances, and one can make oneself understood by it. In a future age, a similar force to that by which wireless telegraphy works will be at human beings' disposal, without any apparatus at all. This will make it possible to cause great devastation at great distances, without anyone being able to discover the origin or cause. These developments will culminate, then eventually implode on themselves.

What is expressed by the Tau is a driving force which can, in contrast, only be set in motion by the power of selfless love. It will be possible to use this power to drive machines—

which will however cease to function if egotistical people make use of them. [. . .] A propelling force that can only be moral is what the future holds: a most important force with which culture must be inoculated if it is not to implode. The mechanical and moral must interpenetrate, since the mechanical is nothing without moral impetus. Today we stand at the threshold of this. In future, machines will be driven not only by water and steam but by spiritual force, by spiritual morality. This power is symbolized by the Tau sign and was indeed poetically symbolized by the image of the Holy Grail. The human being is no longer merely dependent on what nature freely gives him to use: he can shape and transform nature, has become a master craftsman of the inanimate. In the same way he will become a master craftsman of what is living. [. . .]

The Masonic art stands at a turning point in its development and has the closest links with the work of the Lodge of the Grail, with what can appear as salvation in the dreadful conflicts raging all around us.

These conflicts are only just beginning. Humanity is unaware that it is dancing on a volcano. But it is so. The revolutions beginning on our earth make a new phase of the royal art necessary. Those who do not drift thoughtlessly through life will know that they need to participate actively in our earth's evolution. From a certain point of view, therefore, this very ancient royal art must assume a new form to stand alongside what is so ancient, in which lies an inexhaustible force. Those who can grasp the new Masonic ideas will strike new sparks from Freemasonry's ancient symbols. [. . .]

Hitherto the royal art has been a male art, and women were excluded from it. Tasks carried on in the Lodges were kept separate from everything related to the family. [. . .] Man by his nature embodies the energy that works on inanimate matter whereas woman is regarded as embodying the living, creative force that develops the human race from its natural basis. This antithesis must be resolved.

What has to be achieved in future can only happen by overcoming everything relying on the old symbols, expressed precisely in what is sexual in nature. [. . .] The old, sexual symbols are what need to be overcome in the broadest sense; then we can discover what in future must be the creative and truly effective principle in the concept of uniting both male and female spiritual forces. The outward manifestation of this advance in Freemasonry is through admission of the female sex.

There is a significant custom in Freemasonry which relates to this. Everyone inducted into the Lodge is given two pairs of gloves. One he puts on himself, the other is to be put on his chosen lady. This is symbolic of the fact that the couple should only touch each other with gloves on, so that sensual impulses have nothing to do with Freemasonry. This is also expressed in another symbol: the apron symbolizes overcoming sexuality, which is as it were covered by the apron. [. . .] The gloves can even be taken off, however, once lower impulses have been conquered by invoking the free spiritual forces of both sexes. Only then will what manifests today in sexuality be finally overcome. When human creation is free, completely free and autonomous, when man and woman work together on the great edifice of humanity, gloves will no longer be needed, for man and woman will be able freely to stretch out their hands to each other so that spirit speaks to spirit and not sensuality to sensuality. This is the great idea that the future holds. [. . .]

V

THE WAR-TORN SOUL AND THE QUEST FOR INTEGRATION

15. Acknowledging Amfortas

Extract from a lecture given in Berlin on 2 July 1913

For me the following is a key passage in its absolute relevance to modern, existential experience and the inner conflicts we all undergo. Steiner here characterizes the soul at war with itself in various ways in the modern age, and advocates a human integrity and reintegration which takes full account of our 'inner Amfortas'—the figure laid low in the Parzival epic by his pain and suffering. Ideals alone are therefore not enough. We must also pay due heed to the failings and passions which show us where inner work has to start. It is not enough merely to suppress desires deep in the human soul and cover them over with an intellectual veneer and the superficial culture our education provides, for at some point what is merely suppressed surfaces with undeniable force and takes its revenge. This is symbolically portrayed in the Parzival epic by the Klingsor–Kundry alliance: between self-absorbed, materialistic intellect and sensual passions. Steiner says that we cannot 'know Parzival' without plumbing the depths of Amfortas's pain. As such this passage prefigures a holistic psychotherapeutic view of the health of the human psyche.

[...] The Holy Grail is surrounded by many, many mysteries. Today, naturally, we can give only a sketchy outline of these mysteries; but it may provide a starting-point for more detailed studies [...]. The Holy Grail, if truly understood, contained everything which characterizes the secrets of the human soul in later times.[24]

Let us consider an initiate of later times who, having freed his I and astral body from his physical and etheric bodies, emerged from them and looked down at them from without; and let us picture what he saw in them. He saw something which could be very disturbing if he had not learnt to understand it thoroughly. And he still sees it today. The physical and etheric bodies are interwoven with something which flows through them like streams or strands running in various directions. As nerve fibres run through the physical body, so the physical body is also interwoven with something finer than the nerves, which occult vision sees as being dead—so that there really is something like a thread of dead substance in the human body. It is condemned to be dead throughout life between birth and death, but during the eastern stage of human evolution it was still living. Yes, one has the experience that in human bodies there is something dead nowadays which once was alive. And one sets out to discover what it really is. 'Dead' is to be understood here in a relative sense; the dead part is still stimulated by its environment, but there are tendencies and currents in the human body which, in comparison with the life that animates it, always have a disposition toward death. We investigate how this has come about, and we find its origin to be as follows.

In ancient times people's souls possessed a certain faculty of clairvoyance, and in the latter part of Egyptian-Chaldean civilization this clairvoyance still existed to such a degree that, when gazing into the starry heavens, people saw not merely the physical stars but also the spiritual beings united with them. And so, in the intermediate state between waking and sleeping, when the human soul gazed into the universe and saw spiritual entities there, the impression it received was different from that made on the modern human soul, when people study science in the modern way or are living mostly in the ordinary consciousness of our times. But all the souls living and embodied today were also incarnated in the Egyptian-Chaldean epoch. All souls today once looked out from their bodies into starry space, took part in the spiritual life of the universe and received its impressions. This sank into our souls and became an intrinsic part of them. All the souls of today once looked out into the universe and received spiritual impressions in the same way as they now receive impressions of sensory colours and sounds. All this is there still, in the depth of our souls, and these souls formed their bodies in accordance with it. But our souls have forgotten these impressions! They are no longer present in modern consciousness. The up-building forces souls used to receive cannot now nurture the body; and so the corresponding part of physical and etheric bodies remains lifeless. If nothing else were to happen, if people went on living with sciences focused merely on the outer physical world, then human beings would increasingly deteriorate—because their souls have forgotten those former impressions of the spiritual world which help revive and renew the physical and etheric bodies.

That is what the candidate for initiation sees today. And he can say to himself that souls are thirsting to vitalize something in their physical and etheric bodies which they have to abandon as lifeless because the impressions they once absorbed do not penetrate into modern consciousness. This is the disturbing sense that the candidate for initiation has today.

Thus there is something in the human being that is withdrawn from the soul's sovereignty. I beg you to take these words very seriously: something in the nature of the human being today is withdrawn from the rule of the soul, something in him is dead in contrast with the life of the organism that surrounds it. And by working upon this dead part, the luciferic and ahrimanic forces exercise a very great influence on human beings, in a particular way. While people can acquire increasing freedom, the luciferic and ahrimanic forces insinuate themselves precisely into the part of the organism which has been withdrawn from the soul's sovereignty. That is why so many people today feel (and quite rightly say they feel) as if there were two souls dwelling within their breast, and as if one of these souls was trying to tear itself away from the other. Much of what modern human beings find so baffling in their inner experience lies in what has just been said. The Holy Grail was and is nothing other than what can so nurture the living portion of the soul that it can become master of the dead part. Mont Salvat, the sanctuary of the Holy Grail, is the school in which one has to learn, for the sake of the living part of the human soul, something that there was naturally no need to learn in the eastern and Egyptian mysteries.

One needs to learn what has to be poured into the still living part of the soul in order to become master of the corrupted part of the physical body, and the part of the soul that has become unconscious. [. . .]

When the medieval initiate tried to present in picture form what he had to learn in order to permeate with new wisdom the part of his soul that had remained living, he spoke of the castle of the Holy Grail and of the new wisdom—which is in fact the 'Grail'—that flows from it. And when he wanted to indicate all that is hostile to this new wisdom, he pointed to another domain wherein dwelt all the beings and forces which make it their task to gain access to the part of the body that has become dead, and to the part of the human soul that has become unconscious. This domain [...] was Chastel Merveille, the focus for all the forces which attack the human being in this part of his body and soul [...].

All this is closely connected with a figure who glimmers across from the Middle Ages as a legendary being, but is well known to anyone acquainted with the nature of the mysteries: a personality who was quite real in the mid-medieval period: Klingsor, the duke of Terra de Labur, a district we can locate in what is now southern Calabria. From there came incursions by the enemies of the Grail, especially towards Sicily. Today, if we tread Sicilian soil and have esoteric sight, we can be aware of the Akashic[25] reverberations of the great Empedocles still present in the atmosphere; and likewise we can still perceive there the evil reverberations of Klingsor, who allied himself from his duchy of Terra de Labur, across the Straits of Messina, with those enemies of the Grail who occupied the fastness known in occultism and in legend as Calot Bobot.

In the middle of the medieval period, Calot Bobot in Sicily was the seat of the goddess called Iblis, the daughter of Eblis; and of all evil unions which have taken place in the earth's evolution between beings in whose souls occult forces work, the one occultists regard as the worst of all was between Klingsor and Iblis, the daughter of Eblis. Iblis's very name reveals her connection with Eblis, and in Muslim tradition Eblis is the figure we call Lucifer. Iblis is a kind of feminine aspect of Eblis, the Muslim Lucifer, and with her the evil magician Klingsor united his own evil arts, through which in the Middle Ages he worked against the Grail. These things have to be expressed in pictures, but they correspond to realities; they cannot be expressed in abstract ideas. And all hostility to the Grail was embodied and enacted in that fastness of Iblis, 'Calot Bobot'. [. . .]

Everything undertaken by a power hostile to the Grail, also leading to the wound of Amfortas, can ultimately be traced back to the alliance which Klingsor contracted with the stronghold of Iblis, Calot Bobot; and all the misery and suffering which Amfortas depicts in the Grail legend is an expression of that pact. For this reason the soul must still armour itself today in the neighbourhood of those locations, for all influences hostile to the Mysteries of the Grail and the advancing evolution of humanity still emanate from them.

Thus we have on the one hand the kingdom of the Grail and on the other the evil kingdom, Chastel Merveille, with all that came from the pact between Klingsor and Iblis playing into it. And here we can see, expressed in wonderfully dramatic form, all that the most independent and innermost of the soul organs, the intellectual or mind-soul,[26] had to endure in the form of attacks from without. [. . .] The whole transformation which took place in the intellectual or mind-soul is portrayed as legend, stands dramatically before us, in the antithesis between 'Mont Salvat' and 'Chastel Merveille'. We feel an echo of all the sufferings and all the conquests of the intellectual soul in the stories connected with the Holy Grail. [. . .]

People who haven't studied these things deeply enough will often ask how someone such as Goethe can, on the one hand, bear within him certain secrets of the human soul, and on the other be so torn by passions—as we find he was if we read his biography. Goethe's nature was indeed inwardly divided. From a superficial perspective his two aspects are hard to reconcile: the great, high-minded soul, on the one hand, who could write great passages in Part 2 of *Faust*, and gave expression to many deep secrets of human nature in the *Fairytale of the Green Snake and the Beautiful Lily*. In some ways one would like to forget everything one knows from biographies of Goethe, and pay homage only to the soul capable of such achievements. On the other hand there appears in Goethe, tormenting him and often causing him pangs of conscience, his other 'human, all-too-human nature'. Such a divided nature could not have existed in earlier times. It has become possible only more recently—because there now exists in human nature something we have already spoken of, the part of the soul that has become unconscious, and the part of the organism that has died. The living part can be so elevated and purified that the impulse which elaborates the *Fairy Tale of the Green Snake and the Beautiful Lily* is nurtured there, while the other part remains susceptible to attacks from the outer world. And the forces described can take up their dwelling there in a way that wars with a person's higher I. [. . .]

That is what is mysterious and so hard to understand in a nature such as Goethe's; but by the same token it brings to light many hidden aspects of the human soul in modern times. The duality of human nature takes hold, in the first place, within the mind soul, so that it divides into those 'two souls', one of which can sink fairly deeply into matter while the other rises towards the spirit.

In the knights of King Arthur's Round Table we find a repetition of all that the candidate for initiation had in a certain sense to experience through the sentient soul, in its battles with monsters and giants.[27] In everything connected with the Holy Grail, on the other hand, we are shown the mind-soul's experiences in more recent times. Everything we must now undergo to make one part of our divided nature strong enough to penetrate into the mysteries of the spiritual worlds in modern times, must be enacted in the consciousness soul. This is the new element that must be added. What needs to be enacted in the consciousness soul is crystallized in the figure of Parzival. All the legends connected with King Arthur and the Round Table depict a repetition of the experiences of earlier ages in the sentient soul; all the legends and narratives which are directly connected with the Holy Grail, apart from Parzival, represent what the mind-soul had to undergo; and all that finds expression in the figure of Parzival, as exemplar of a more modern kind of initiation, represents the forces which we have to acquire through the consciousness soul. So the interaction of the three soul principles in modern human beings is presented as legend in a threefold form. And just as we can discern deep secrets of the human soul in old legends, so can we now also sense in them deep secrets of the mysteries of the modern age.

[...] The whole nature of modern initiation has a more inward character than ancient initiation practices, and makes greater demands on the innermost part of the human soul; but in a certain sense it cannot directly approach the external aspect of human nature. Much more than in the old initiation, therefore, what is external must be cleansed and purified by strengthening the inner, so that this inner aspect becomes lord over the outer. Asceticism and external training belong more to the character of the old initiation, whereas direct development of the soul itself, to evolve strong inner forces, belongs more to modern initiation. And because external circumstances are such that the lifeless elements of human nature can only gradually be overcome—the elements which can so greatly disturb or hamper a modern initiate—we must say that in our time and on into the far future there will still be many divided natures similar to Goethe: people who rise up into the heights in one part of their being, while with the other part they remain entangled in the 'human, all-too-human'. [. . .]

The reverberating effects of Klingsor and Iblis are still always present, even though in a different form.

A special feature of our time is that these attacks from Klingsor and Iblis, as they gradually take hold of people, insinuate themselves into intellectual life, particularly the intellectual life that bears on education, with its popularization of modern science. Consider what people have been learning for quite a long time now and what they think it right to instil into children; consider what is accepted as the basis of modern education. [. . .] All this should be judged in terms of how it influences and is impressed on the soul. When someone becomes cleverer and cleverer, in the sense in which it is fashionable to call people clever today, he develops certain forces in his soul which, in this incarnation, may render him very acute when discussing materialistic ideas; yet certain vital forces necessary for the human organism are worn away. And when such a person has absorbed only these, typical, dregs of modern education, in his next incarnation he will lack the forces required to properly build up the human organism. The 'cleverer' a person is by the standards of our day, and the closer his intellectual attunement to it, the more of an imbecile will he be in a later incarnation. Those categories and concepts which relate only to the sense-perceptible outer world and to the ideas which constitute it, set up a configuration in the soul which may be ever so fine intellectually but lack the force to work intensively on the brain [in a future incarnation] and to make use of it; and to be unable to make use of the brain while in the physical body is to be an imbecile.

If it were true, as materialists maintain, that our brain does the thinking, then one could certainly offer them some comfort. But this is as false as the assertion that the 'speech-centre' has evolved by itself. It has acquired its form through human beings learning to speak, and thus the speech-centre is the *result* of speech. Similarly, all cerebral activity, even in the historical past, is the result of thinking—not the other way about. The brain is modelled and formed through thinking. If only such thoughts are developed as are customary today, if they are not permeated by wisdom of the spirit, then souls occupied with thinking only about material things will find in later incarnations that they are unable to use their brains properly; their brain forces will be too weak. A soul pre-occupied today merely with calculating debit and credit, let us say, or with commercial and industrial life, or one that absorbs only the ideas of materialistic science, fills itself with thought-pictures which in later incarnations gradually darken consciousness, because the brain would become an unformed mass—as can happen today in cases of softening of the brain—and so no longer capable of acting as an instrument for the forces of thinking. Hence anyone who looks into these deeper forces of human evolution will see that everything in the soul must be permeated by a spiritual outlook.

So in our modern age human nature continues to be divided. The forces belonging in particular to the consciousness soul must be infused with inner spiritual knowledge. Human beings must battle with the two spheres which Parzival traversed, overcoming 'dullness' and 'doubt' in their own soul. If they were to carry dullness and doubt with them into a later incarnation, they would not make a success of it. Human beings must come to knowledge of the worlds of spirit. Only when life expands in the human soul, the life which Wolfram von Eschenbach calls *Saelde* or blessedness—the life that imbues the consciousness soul with spiritual knowledge—can human soul development advance fruitfully from the fifth epoch towards the sixth.

[...] Unlike all ancient mystery wisdom, these fruits of the modern mysteries can be understood by the generality of people. The unconscious and dead forces of the soul and of the organism must gradually be overcome through permeation of the consciousness soul with spiritual knowledge; that is, with a knowledge that has been understood and grasped spiritually, not a knowledge dependent on authority. [...]

Now it may perhaps be true for many people today who seek knowledge of higher worlds that their outer life will still show aspects of the 'human, all-too-human', or of their efforts to transcend this. Yes, it may well be that the 'fool's motley' is still discernible through the raiment of the spiritual, as was true of Parzival. But that is not the point. What matters is that the impulse towards spiritual knowledge, spiritual understanding, should be present in the soul: that impulse which is inextinguishable in Parzival and brings him at last, despite everything, to the stronghold of the Holy Grail. In the whole picture drawn of Parzival, if rightly understood, we can find all the different methods of training the consciousness soul, which are necessary to evoke from it the right effects, so that one can gain control of the forces which whirl in confusion and war with one another in the mind-soul today. The more that we look inwards today and try to exercise honest self-knowledge, the more we will find conflict raging in the soul; this is a conflict within the intellectual or mind-soul. Self-knowledge is a harder thing than many people suppose, and it will indeed become ever more difficult. We try to acquire self-knowledge, but even if we manage to discipline ourselves in many respects and develop our character, we can still frequently find, at critical moments, the most deeply hidden passions and forces raging in our innermost depths, rending apart the domain of the mind-soul.

And how is it for someone today who devotes himself seriously to knowledge and the pursuit of knowledge? The difficulties of the inner life may perhaps never dawn on people who believe that real knowledge is to be found in external science and its fruits. But anyone who takes the quest for knowledge seriously and with worthy motives will look with real insight into his own inner being. He seeks continually in this or that field of knowledge, and seeks also to come to terms with diverse aspects of human life. After searching for a while, he thinks he knows something; but then he searches further. And the more he searches with the means normally available today, the more he feels torn apart, and assailed by doubt. Someone who, having acquired a modern education, confesses to himself that despite all this education he really knows nothing, is often the very person who most earnestly and worthily seeks for spiritual knowledge.

There can be no one with any depth of soul today who does not experience this gnawing doubt. And it is something we should be familiar with. For only then will we immerse ourselves in the spiritual knowledge which is right for the consciousness soul and must pour itself out into the mind-soul so as to be sovereign there. So we must try to penetrate with rational understanding what esoteric knowledge presents to the consciousness soul. By this means we will draw into our inner being a self that will be a real lord and master there; and then we can confront ourselves fully in the modern mysteries.

Anyone who approaches these mysteries today must feel that he is confronting and challenging himself by striving for the virtues of Parzival, while knowing that—because of modern conditions already described and because he is a modern human being—he is in fact someone else also, the wounded Amfortas. Today we bear this divided nature within us: aspiring Parzival, wounded Amfortas. That is what self-knowledge must lead us to feel. From this recognition will flow the forces which make a unity again of this duality, and will thus advance us a little further in world evolution. In our mind-soul, in the depths of our inner life, Amfortas, wounded in body and soul, must meet Parzival, whose task is to cultivate the consciousness soul. And it is entirely true to say that in order to gain his freedom a person must undergo the 'wounding' of Amfortas and become acquainted with the Amfortas within, so that he may also come to know Parzival. [. . .] A wish to deny our Amfortas nature is not in tune with our times. Modern people try to deny Amfortas because they are so fond of surrounding themselves with maya, with illusions. How fine it sounds to say that 'humanity is always progressing!' Yes, but such 'progress' follows a very tortuous path. And to develop the forces of Parzival in human nature, our wounded Amfortas nature must be acknowledged. [. . .]

16. The Word in Chains

Extract from a lecture given in Dornach on 11 March 1923

In the previous excerpt Steiner refers to the evolution of the human brain and the very detrimental effect on future incarnations that materialistic thinking in this life will have. In the following passage he takes this theme further, giving a vivid picture of our loss of contact with angelic realms in sleep through the reverberation in us of materialistic thoughts and words. Steiner evokes the prosaic nature of today's ordinary speech, adapted to modern conditions, which loses its power to lift us beyond the mundane and instead 'fetters the soul to the murmurings of the physical world'. Though this passage makes no mention of the Grail, it offers, as it were, a shadow or counter-image of it: the sundering of people both from each other and from worlds of spirit.

The element of soul we instil into our words from morning to evening continues to vibrate and pulse from the moment of going to sleep until the moment of waking. We are unconscious of it, but let me assure you that everything spoken during the day echoes on—admittedly in reverse order—during sleep. Not that the words actually sound again as they sound through our mouth during the day; it is, rather, the undulation of feeling in the words that resounds, the will impetus that has flowed into them, the gaiety or sadness, the joy or pain expressed and revealed in the flow of speech. [. . .]

Now a characteristic of our epoch is that it produces more and more individuals who take with them into sleep something which actually hinders their souls from understanding the speech of the archangeloi; and the archangeloi find no pleasure in the echoes of speech reverberating from these individuals during sleep.

The era has begun—we have to use earthly terms in speaking of these things, which are naturally difficult to speak of in ordinary language—when the beings of the world of spirit can no longer come to any real understanding with sleeping human souls, when misunderstandings keep occurring between what the beings of the spiritual hierarchies say and what echoes in human souls during sleep. Discrepancies and disharmonies creep in.

This is the aspect which reveals itself in our era when viewed from the other side of life: a tormenting condition of misunderstanding, of complete lack of understanding between human souls and spiritual beings has insinuated itself into the state of sleep. And the question as to the reason for this condition must weigh heavily on those who are aware of a spiritual fact such as this.

The words we draw from the range of our native language may, while we learn them in childhood, develop in a way that applies to the physical world alone. This has increasingly been the case in the age of materialism. Words are available but these words only express what is physical in nature. In former times, in contrast, a human being became so intimate with language that there were many words whose content transported him into worlds of spirit. It has to be admitted that true idealism has become feeble in our time, particularly in those who absorb modern intellectual culture.

It makes a great difference whether ideals are or are not embodied in the language we use. Students today may certainly have a feeling for words which refer to solid, external, material things; but when it is a matter of rising to the level of pure thoughts that reflect spiritual realities, they stop thinking at once and the threads of their thought are broken. This is true particularly of those who are considered well-educated by modern standards, when they try to assimilate the idealistic concepts of pure thinking. The words seem to be no more than semblance. It is a fact that today children grow up with a language whose words have no wings to carry them away from earthly conditions.

In the first phase of life, until the age of seven or so, the child during sleep can still experience the spiritual realm through the echoes of speech emanating from his human environment. If materialism causes this environment to repudiate the spirit, it is repudiating itself, for it consists of both soul and spirit. But during the first phase of life the human being during sleep is still able to experience the spiritual.

This continues during the second phase of life from the age of 7 to 14. But if, eventually, there is no longer any idealistic, spiritual significance in the words used around the young human being—as may well happen in this materialistic age when religious ideas have lost their strong spiritual influence on human souls—then, after the age of 14, with the onset of puberty, a young person enters a phase of soul life that chains him to the physical during sleep. The echoes of spoken language then coerce the soul and confine it to the physical realm. The reverberations of the mineral world resonate from all directions into what the human being experiences between falling sleep and waking; so, too, do the reverberations of the physical content of the plant world. This brings discord into the echoes of speech: the soul cannot then elaborate what the genius of speech otherwise imparts to language, which can bring about understanding between the human soul and the beings of the higher hierarchies.

And then a strange condition arises. The soul experiences something but cannot express it, because it is not consciously experienced. What the soul experiences may be characterized roughly as follows: after puberty, when the human being enters the world of spirit in sleep, the world of the archangeloi opens out before him: he senses it but no threads of thought pass from that world into his soul or from his soul into that world. And on waking he comes back into the physical world having suffered this tragic deprivation. [. . .]

Speech is being divested of everything that enhances descriptive power, rhythm, measure, melody, dramatic effect—that is to say, everything that leads it back into the realm of the soul, where the imaginative element lifts it into the world of spirit. In language, we find, increasing concessions are made to materialism.

Language as it exists today among all civilized peoples fetters the soul during sleep to the purely physical murmurings of the mineral world, to the rustlings of the purely physical content of the plant world, and no longer enables the clear speech of the angeloi and the resounding trumpet tones of the archangeloi, with their profound significance, to be audible to the soul.

From puberty onwards, the human being today ought to bring with him into sleep an element of speech that has prepared his brain during waking hours to understand the ideal content of what is expressed in words. He ought to be able to bring with him—for the speech of the archangeloi *can* be heard by his soul during the hours of sleep—something that enables his circulating blood to experience, to some degree at least, the spiritual depths of cosmic occurrences. And if he cannot acquire spiritual knowledge today, if our school education is not spiritually deepened, he will bring with him instead the rumbling sounds of the physical, mineral world; and will also bring with him, in his blood, the rustling, thudding sounds of the physical aspect of the plant world.

Through conventional speech he thus becomes dependent on his mineralized brain that is disharmonious in sleep, and on the blood system with the hissing and rustling sounds surging through it; and so he is confined through speech to life in the earthly sphere alone, whereas in other circumstances words could have borne him above merely earthly experience to experience in a higher realm.

How can individuals who have been exposed to today's materialistic education still affirm, from the depths of their souls, that 'Thought is my boundless realm and my winged instrument is the Word'?[28] For people today thought is by no means any longer a 'boundless' but a strictly circumscribed realm, embracing only material objects in the environment. And the word is no winged instrument, but one by means of which we stammer from mouth to ear the vague utterances of our inner life, but in a way that contains little spiritual significance. Whereas a spiritual world view could be an ocean into which our inner being sinks, and which could then lift our soul to ever greater heights, it becomes instead the means of chaining us to the earth in a straitjacket of earthly existence.

Today this state of affairs is affecting the destiny of the whole human race. We can see how modern civilization is based on differences between people throughout the globe, as expressed in their languages. Because of the way language has developed, it is evident that cultural divisions and ideas are concerned with purely material life, that they form, as it were, a covering spread in the guise of civilization over all the peoples of the earth in order to shut them off from the world of spirit. Everywhere today we see this wall of materialism built around the human soul, and it is this that also imbues external life with materialistic attitudes of thinking and feeling. It is this that gradually causes people to forget that conditions within the human race are determined from supersensible spheres. When humanity is divided into nations, races and so on, people become increasingly imbued with a blind belief that they must persist in a purely materialistic existence. [...]

A spiritual knowledge of human existence is essential, the world view of spiritual science. This must therefore permeate the whole of education so that, instead of acquiring a store of words from which all wings have been removed, the child absorbs and is guided by the spirit and receives, together with the words, the power that raises him into the spiritual worlds in which his being is rooted. In physical life we can deny the spirit. With the spiritual part of our being, which has to lay aside the physical and etheric bodies during sleep, we cannot deny the spirit. And if we repudiate the spirit from the physical side of existence, then we wake up each morning as adults who no longer understand life; and this lack of understanding imbues all our thinking, feeling and will. [...] The evolution of language to its present condition has reached a point where, when people should rightly associate with spiritual beings, they inevitably remain deaf and dumb and can absorb only what drags them down—the physical element of the mineral and plant kingdoms. To understand life today—to use a banal expression—we need to look behind and beyond the scenes of this life. But only through genuine spiritual science is this possible.

17. Balancing the Soul

Extract from a lecture given in The Hague on 26 March 1913

Steiner here reiterates the need for us to achieve a balance and harmony in our souls by reconciling our inner Amfortas and inner Parzival. The former infuses his interest in the world with too much personal desire while the latter, to begin with at least, is too uninterested in and disengaged from life around him to express compassion. We therefore have a dynamic here which suggests a pendulum swing between the two extremes of excessive control and disengagement, neither of which are truly free. Between them the Christ holds sway and can help us first recognize then gradually achieve an inner poise and balance.

[. . .] The astral body is somewhat detached and independent in the case of esotericists, or those who seriously engage in anthroposophical inner development and who place spiritual knowledge at the centre of their lives. [. . .]

What is called love may at times be very egotistic or self-serving. But an egotism that extends beyond the person may also become very disinterested—that is, it may cherish what it owns and devotedly protect it. We learn from such examples (as a mother protecting her child or a farmer tending his crops) that life cannot be circumscribed by abstract concepts. We speak of egotism and altruism, and can devise very fine theories based on such notions. Reality however is not confined within such systems; when egotism extends its interest so that it considers its environment as part of itself, cherishing and nurturing it, then egotism can become selflessness. On the other hand, altruism may try to make the whole world happy by imposing its own preferences, its thoughts and feelings, at all costs, and may come to act on the grim presumption that if you don't wish to show me fellow feeling I'll crack your skull! Thus altruism can become extremely egotistic. [...]

We may describe the astral body as an egotist. This means that every path of development that aims to liberate the astral body must recognize the interests of humanity by expanding and becoming progressively wider in scope. Indeed, before the astral body can liberate itself properly from the other bodies, it must become interested in the whole earth and all humanity. The interests of humanity must become our interests; our interests must no longer be associated in any way with what is personal. [...]

The purpose of the Grail legend is to penetrate into the inmost depths of the astral body, into its archetypal interests because, if left to itself, the astral body becomes an egotist and considers only its most innate, selfish interests.

We can diverge in only two directions where the astral body is concerned, tending towards Amfortas before he was fully redeemed; or to Parzival. As far as the astral body is concerned, proper human development lies between the two. The astral body develops forces of egotism in itself, but is undermined if, instead of extending its interests to embrace the whole earth, these interests are limited to a single, separate personality. This should not happen because then the whole human personality is wounded by the ego force expressed in the blood; in others words, we make the mistake of Amfortas.

Amfortas's basic error is to introduce personal wishes and desires, which then persist, into the sphere of the astral body's rightful, extended egotism and interest in the world.

As soon as we bring personal interests into the sphere where the astral body must overcome them, a suffering is introduced that will not heal; and we become the wounded Amfortas.

The other error may also lead us astray, and can be avoided only if the person exposed to such misfortune is as innocent as Parzival. Parzival sees the Grail pass repeatedly before him; and he too makes a grave error, though one of omission. Each time the Grail passes before him it is on the tip of his tongue to ask who this food is really intended for; but the question dies on his lips and finally the meal ends without his asking the question. Then, after the meal, he withdraws without taking an opportunity to make good his omission.

This is as if someone—not yet fully developed—were to become momentarily clairvoyant during the night, as if separated by an abyss from what is contained in the citadel of the body; and, after briefly contemplating it without having gained the necessary knowledge (that is, without asking the requisite question), discovering that everything has closed again around the moment of clairvoyant vision, shutting him out. Even after waking, such a person would be unable to re-enter the citadel. What was it that Parzival actually failed to do?

We have mentioned that the Holy Grail contains the substance that nourishes the physical instrument of the earthly human being: the pure mineral essence derived from food that, in the purest part of the human brain, unites with the finest sense impressions.[29] To whom should this food be served? [. . .] The Grail must be offered to the one who comes to understand the maturity needed to lift himself gradually and with increasing awareness to knowledge of what the

Grail is. But how does one attain the capacity to lift oneself consciously to the Holy Grail?

The poem clearly indicates who the Holy Grail is intended for. [. . .] In the original legend, the lord of the castle is the Fisher King, in other words a king ruling over fisher folk. This can remind us of someone else who lived among fisher folk too, but did not try to be their king. He wanted a different relationship to them, brought them something other than royal dominion over them. This was Jesus Christ. This can show us that the error of the Fisher King, or Amfortas in the original legend, is this: Amfortas is not fully worthy to receive healing through the Grail because he tries to rule over his fisher folk by force. He does not wish to allow the spirit alone to govern them.

Initially Parzival is insufficiently attentive or awake to ask, in full self-awareness, 'What is the purpose of the Grail?'

What does this question require? It requires the Fisher King to uproot his personal, self-focused interest and enlarge this interest to embrace all humanity in imitation of Christ Jesus. Parzival, on the other hand, must raise his interest above that of a mere innocent spectator to an inner understanding of the commonality of all human beings; to humanity's rightful gift of the Holy Grail. Thus in a wonderful way Christ, the original Fisher King, hovers between Parzival and Amfortas. At the turning point in the legend there is a subtle hint that the Fisher King has, on the one hand, introduced too much personality into the spheres of the astral body; and that, on the other, Parzival has not shown enough interest in the general affairs of humanity and is still too naïve, too unresponsive to world concerns.

The tremendous educational value of the Grail legend lay in its capacity to allow those who followed it to perceive a kind of balance or scale: between what Amfortas represented on the one hand, and on the other what Parzival represented. They could thus recognize that a balance needed to be established. If the astral body pursues its innate, original interests, it will rise to the ideal of universal humanity expressed in the words, 'Where two or three are gathered together in my name, there am I in the midst of them'.

VI

THE GRAIL IN THE HUMAN ORGANISM: SPIRIT INFUSING MATTER

18. From Dullness to Inner Joy

Extract from a lecture given in Dornach on 22 October 1922

The passages in this section take some of the previous observations one stage further by locating them in the physical nature of the human organism. The Grail is not merely some nebulous or invisible emanation from a dimly comprehended sphere, but something that can and does work right into the very tissue of physical life, even having its seat or 'castle' in the physical body. In other words, the spirit works deeply into matter and its signs can be found and nurtured wherever the fire of enthusiasm penetrates torpidity.

If we do not restrict ourselves to looking at a God who is distinct and separate but instead follow God into His specific activities, we will arrive at what humanity needs for the future. Otherwise humanity will ultimately nurture only the abstract and will arrive at a purely materialistic science. Only if we can penetrate to the actual details of how substances work within divine creation will we arrive at a point where we can penetrate religion with science and lead science back to religion.

You see, around the twelfth, thirteenth and fourteenth centuries a view arose in Europe that I have already characterized from different angles. It is expressed in the legend of the Grail, the Parzival legend—in all that has been written by poets such as Wolfram von Eschenbach, Hartmann von Aue, and Gottfried von Strassburg. The motifs surface there. In the Parzival epic, the true Parzival epic, one motif surfaces particularly: of how the human being needs to develop towards what was called *Saelde* at the time. This is a certain inner sense of joy—*Saelde*—close to what we might call bliss or blessedness, but not quite the same. *Saelde* means to be penetrated with a certain inner sense of joy. This motif surfaces and in fact dominates European culture in the thirteenth and fourteenth centuries. All poetic motifs, and also all prose motifs—particularly the Parzival motif—are pervaded by this, and everything strives towards it. One strives towards this *Saelde,* this inner sense of joy: it is not unreligious, nor simply comfortable inner happiness but is really the state of being ensouled by the Creator's divine forces.

Why does this come about? It arises in fact through the transition from kidney to liver activity in the human being. Physiology can help us understand this. Earlier physiologists were, of course, better physiologists in a certain sense than the materialistic physiologists of today. By 'early physiologists' I really mean the writers of the Old Testament who said of bad dreams, for example: 'The Lord punished me last night through my kidneys.' This knowledge of certain connections between abnormal kidney activity and bad dreams persisted; and in the eighth, ninth and tenth centuries, for instance, people were still deeply convinced that kidney activity makes one heavy. People felt that the kidney had gradually acquired something of a heavy quality. [...] Permeation of the organism with bile, in contrast, was connected with *Saelde* quality, with an experience of deliverance, inner deliverance. It was experienced as an inner yet divinely permeated feeling of bliss, a striving away from the dullness of the kidney. The kidney also develops a thinking activity, a dull thinking activity mediated by the system of ganglia which is then connected in turn to the spinal cord and the brain system. It develops in particular the kind of thinking that also played a role in the Middle Ages. At that time it was called mental 'dullness' (*Tumpfheit*). And this development from *Tumpfheit* to *Saelde*—to illumined bliss—became the motif of Parzival. Parzival develops from *Tumpfheit* to *Saelde*, from dullness to inner joy.

One must not consider this only in an abstract way but also with feeling and sensitivity. To start with it seems that Parzival arises from a culture that has grown heavy and dull. It is hard for him to get into dynamic movement. Only later, after passing through doubt, is he permeated with inner joy. Doubt is within him, thoroughly shaking him up in the heart-lung system. After passing through this state he finds access to inner joy or *Saelde*.

It is possible to trace the broader history and evolution of the world in the human organism. We can say that leading individuals, such as those who fashioned the Parzival motif, were pioneers and the first precursors of this modern organization of humanity, making the transition from the kidney activity of the past to a newer type of liver activity.

This is not something to be ridiculed. One should not say that these things are just embedded in lower, physical and sensory nature. God after all did not scorn to create 'lower' matter. He created it! By the same token, knowledge obliges us to pursue the divine activity of the Creator into the furthest reaches of the material world, [. . .] and even the physiological activity at work in the human being.

The world is a unity: one can descend from what must be seen as the loftiest religious ideas to something that people often regard as being so lowly that they do not want to consider it. [. . .]

It can be said that food is absorbed, broken down, reconfigured, astralized, transformed into I-hood—and only then does one understand ptyalin or pepsin in the food we eat: it is absorbed, broken down and then transported into the lymph glands, conveyed to the heart, fired by the heart and irradiated by the kidneys; everything is then made astral, taken up by the liver function and conveyed to the I. Then all of this can be 'compiled' by spleen activity and under certain circumstances this will fire a person with enthusiasm, will give him strength from the world of spirit, mediated by spleen activity; or, through spleen activity, a person may become full of 'spleen', moody and depressed. Then he is someone who just wants to sit about idly, unthinking, and would much prefer not to be fired by the spirit. There are many people like this today. They drive one to despair like heavy lumps, as if they had no heads at all. Spleen activity, which could be something lofty in the human being, actually has a crushing effect on such people. They develop 'spleen' instead of enthusiasm, as can be seen today in all kinds of forms.

What one needs today however is the kind of work that transforms as much spleen as possible into enthusiasm and fire, so that human culture wakes up rather than dozing. This is in fact what anthroposophy should kindle: to be wide awake, to be enthusiastic, to transform knowledge into real activity, into deeds, so that the human being not only *knows* something but *becomes* something through anthroposophy. [...]

19. The Fire of Compassion

Extract from a lecture given in Prague on 28 March 1911

This short but radiant passage is like a continuation and culmination of the previous excerpt's final paragraph. Though the Grail is not mentioned, the idea of developing warmth and compassion for all beings and creatures is at the very heart of the 'Parzival project'.

What the organism produces in the way of inner warmth processes in our blood, warmth processes which it conducts to us through all its different processes, and which it finally brings to expression in a flowering of all other processes, penetrates up into the soul and spirit, transforms itself into soul and spirit. The most beautiful, the loftiest thing about it is the fact that, through the forces of the human soul, what is organic in nature can be metamorphosed into soul nature! If everything we can possess through the activity of our earthly organism is rightly transformed by us after it has become warmth, it then transmutes itself in the soul into what we may call an inner, living experience of compassion, an interest in all other beings. If we penetrate through all the processes of the human organism to the highest level of all, to the processes of warmth, we pass, as it were, through the door of human physiological processes ... into the world where the warmth of the blood gains worth in relation to what our soul makes of it, to the extent that the soul develops living interest for all existence, and compassion for everything around it. In this way, if our inner life carries us on to a kindling of inner heat, we broaden our life beyond all earthly existence. And we must comprehend the wonderful fact that the whole of cosmic existence has first taken the roundabout path of developing our whole organism in order finally to give us that warmth we must transmute through our I into living compassion for all beings.

In the earth's mission, warmth is in the process of being transmuted into compassion.

This is the meaning of earth evolution; and it is being fulfilled . . . through the fact that all physical processes finally come together in our organism as their crown; that everything in it, as a microcosm of all earthly processes, opens again into new blossoming. And as this is transmuted in the human soul, our interest and living compassion for every kind of being enables the earth organism to attain the goal for which warmth was assigned us as beings on earth. What we absorb into our souls through living interest, helping us broaden our inner soul life more and more, will accompany us as we pass through many transformations* so that we can use to the full, for the spirit, all that the earth can give us as kindling heat, burning warmth, flame of fire!

---

* Steiner is referring to reincarnation: the repeated rebirth of the individual human spirit in different epochs of evolution.

20. Raising Earthly Substance

Extracts from two lectures given in Dornach on
9 and 10 November 1923

Just as Parzival must come to act entirely out of himself and connect individually with the Grail, so physical processes in us can be raised through our own inner warmth to receive and sustain a spiritual influx.

If we study the human metabolic system in isolation [. . .] we find it constantly tending to make us ill, in all sorts of ways. The origin of internal diseases—not those caused by external injury—must always be sought in the metabolic system. A rational observation of diseases must therefore start with the metabolic system, and every metabolic phenomenon needs to be addressed with the question: which route are you taking? [. . .] To each individual process the question must be put: 'What is it that you really want?' And it will answer: 'On my own I am a process that always causes illness.' [. . .]

Thus if you wish to gain an idea of how a mineral substance is utilized in the human being, you must say the following [diagram drawn]: here is the mineral substance; this mineral substance enters into us. It passes through the fluid state and is transformed into warmth ether. This warmth ether has a strong disposition to absorb into itself what radiates inwards, streams inwards, as forces from cosmic spaces, from the breadths of the cosmos. Thus it absorbs the forces of the cosmos. And these forces of the universe now become the spiritual forces which here imbue warmth-etherized earthly matter with spirit. And only then, with the help of this warmth-etherized earthly substance, does there enter into the body what it needs to take shape and form.

So you see that if, as people once did, we designate heat or warmth as the element of fire, we can say that what we absorb in the way of mineral substance is raised to the level where it assumes the nature of fire in us. And what is of the nature of fire has the disposition to absorb the influences of the higher hierarchies; and then this fire streams back again into all our internal regions and resolidifies to provide the material basis for individual organs. Nothing that human beings take into themselves remains as it is; nothing remains earthly. [. . .]

You see, everything in the external world is poison for us, actual poison; and it only becomes of service to us when, through our own individual forces, we lay hold of it and make it our own. For only from the human being himself do forces ascend to the higher hierarchies in a human way. [. . .]

We must work on the mineral until it becomes warmth ether in order that it may absorb the spiritual; then, after the mineral has absorbed the spiritual, the human being can be built up by it. [. . .]

21. Raying In, and Raying Out from Within

Extract from a lecture given in Dornach on 16 May 1920

In the warmth-related 'evaporation of substance' that occurs in thinking, we are, says Steiner, very slowly transmuting ourselves and the whole earth into a new form. He invokes the dual image of the Grail and Parzival as the point of transition in us between what we receive as spiritual perception and what we give out again ourselves through our own powers. This is also the point where thinking passes from the insubstantiality of pictures to the new and newly creative substance and reality of the human spirit. In other words—and this is a striking thought—one could say that the Grail's efficacy and Parzival's engagement with it are mutually interdependent, as each other's ultimate fulfilment. The one only acquires its full reality as the inner, individual possession of the other. This is symbolically depicted in the Parzival saga when the name of Parzival appears in shining letters on the golden vessel.

If we study the idea of the human being in a real way, we find that the thinking which asserts itself in our head has a great deal to do with the inner activity associated with conditions of heat and warmth. [. . .] It is evident that something like a cooperation of thought activity and warmth activity takes place. What does this consist of? Here we come to something which requires very careful consideration.

First taking the whole of the rest of the human being, and then his head, we can of course trace metabolism from the former to the latter; and the fact that ultimately the head has to do with thinking can be sensed as a direct experience. Yet what really happens here? We will lead to this gradually, and eventually arrive at a fitting picture of what happens. Let us suppose we have a fluid substance; we bring it to boiling point, then it evaporates and changes into a more rarefied substance. This same process takes place far more intensely with human thinking, whose effect on metabolism in the human head is to make all substance fall away like a sediment and be expelled, so that nothing remains of it but mere *picture*.

I will now use another image to make things clear. Suppose you have a vessel containing a solution. This you cool down, which is again a heat process. A sediment collects below, and above remains finer liquid. This is also the case with the human head; only here no substance whatever is collected above, nothing but pictures, all matter is expelled. This is the activity of the human head: it forms what are mere pictures, and expels what is matter. This process in fact takes place in everything that may be called our transition to pure thinking. All material substance that has been active in our inner life falls back, as it were, into the organism, and pictures alone remain. It is a fact that when we rise to pure thought we live in pictures. Our soul lives in pictures; and these pictures are the remains of all that has preceded them. Not the substance, but the pictures remain. [. . .]

The nature of the instinctive wisdom of the ancients was such that it did not filter out matter in this way. This filtering away of all matter and substance is a result of human evolution. Although not acknowledged by external physiology, it is generally true that the thinking of humanity before the Mystery of Golgotha was always united with matter, and that at the time when the Mystery of Golgotha intervened in the life and evolution of the earth, humanity had evolved to a point where it could separate out matter from the inner process of thought—matter-free thought became possible.

Please don't think this is unimportant! It is actually one of the most important things of all that in our evolution we have become free from corporeal thinking, that thoughts have changed to pure pictures. [. . .] Since the Mystery of Golgotha, the universe has as it were withdrawn. We have been transposed to an existence which only unfolds in pictures. [. . .]

Before the Mystery of Golgotha [. . .] all human beings felt the starry heavens streaming into them; and they felt this above all as a group, as a community of people into whom the starry heavens rayed. In the evolution of Hebrew antiquity we can discover a time when the 12 tribes of Jacob were seen as a projection on earth of the 12 regions of heaven. [. . .] We find something similar later on in the Middle Ages, if we study the legends of King Arthur and his Round Table. [. . .] There was however a difference. Hebrew antiquity evolved to a point where this instreaming from the cosmos still yielded corporeal or matter-imbued pictures. Then came the point when the body withdrew from such pictures, when they had to receive a new substantiality. There was indeed a danger that human soul life would pass entirely into a life of pictures or images. People did not immediately recognize this danger. Even Descartes was still floundering, and instead of saying, 'I think therefore I am not,' he said the opposite of the truth: 'I think, therefore I am.' When we live in pictures, we really are not! When we live in mere thoughts this is the surest sign that we are not. Thoughts must be filled with substantiality. In order that the human being should not continue to live in mere pictures, in order that inner substantiality might once more exist in us, the being intervened who entered through the Mystery of Golgotha. Hebrew antiquity was the first to meet with this intervention of the core power which was to give back reality to the human soul that had become picture. This however was not understood immediately. In the Middle Ages we have the last echoes of this in the 12 around King Arthur's table; but this was soon replaced by something else—the Parzival legend, which contrasts a single human being with the 12: one person who develops twelvefoldness out of his own inner core.

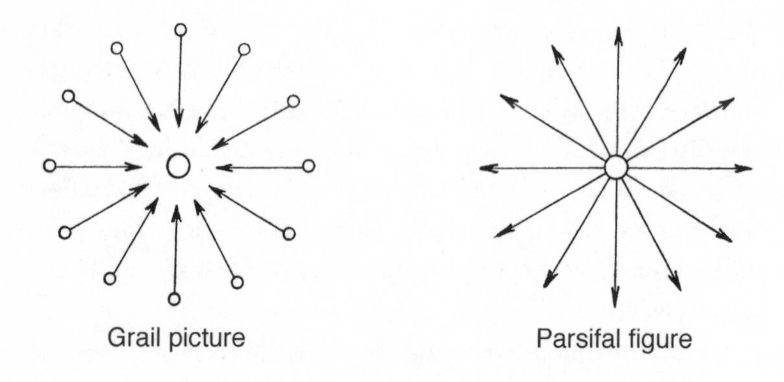

Thus in contrast to that first picture (left diagram), which was essentially that of the Grail, must be set the Parzival picture (right diagram) in which what the human being now possesses within him rays out from the centre. The endeavour of those in the Middle Ages who wished to understand Parzival, who wished to make the Parzival striving active in the human soul, was to introduce true substantiality, inner reality, into the image life in the human being that crystallizes out after all materiality has filtered away. Whereas the Grail legend still shows an instreaming into the centre from without, the Parzival figure is now set against this, raying out an inner life from the centre that can restore reality to mere pictures.

The Parzival legend thus represented the striving of humanity in the Middle Ages to find the way to the Christ within. It represents an instinctive striving to understand what lives as Christ in humanity's evolution. If one studies what was experienced through this figure of Parzival, and compares it with what is to be found in creeds and faiths, one receives a strong impulse towards what needs to happen today. People are now satisfied with the mere husk of the word 'Christ', believing that this in itself is enough, a possession, whereas even theologians themselves do not possess Him but remain at the level of more superficial, external interpretation and exegesis. In the Middle Ages, enough direct perception was left so that, by comprehending the representative of humanity, Parzival, people were able to wrest their way upwards to the figure of Christ. If we reflect on this we also gain a sense of our whole place in the universe. Throughout the natural world, conversion and transformation of forces and energy prevails. In the human being alone matter is cast out by pure thought. The matter cast out of the human being by pure thought is also annihilated, passing into nothingness. In us, therefore, is a place in the universe where matter ceases to exist.

If we think about this, we must think of all life on earth as follows. Here is the earth, and on the earth the human being; into us matter passes. Everywhere else it is transmuted, transformed. In us it is annihilated. The material earth will pass away as matter is gradually destroyed in us. When, some day, all the earth's substance has passed through the human organism, being used there for thinking, the earth will cease to be a planetary body. And what human beings will have gained from this earth are pictures. These, however, will have a new reality, will preserve a primal reality. This reality is the one proceeding from the core power which entered human evolution through the Mystery of Golgotha. Looking towards the end of our earth, therefore, what do we see? The end of the earth will come when all its substance is destroyed as described above. The human being will then possess pictures of all that has occurred in human evolution. At the end of earth evolution, without the Mystery of Golgotha, the earth would have been absorbed back into the universe, and there would remain pictures without reality. What makes them real, however, is that the Mystery of Golgotha actually took place within earth evolution, giving these pictures inner reality for the life to come. Through the Mystery of Golgotha, a new beginning becomes possible for the earth's future existence. [. . .]

We have not grasped Christianity until we can say to ourselves: precisely in the domain of heat a change is taking place in us which results in matter being destroyed and a purely picture existence arising out of matter; but through the union of the human soul with the Christ substance, this picture existence becomes a new reality. [. . .]

We do not participate only in the evolving material universe, but in its decay too; and we are now in the process of raising ourselves out of it to mere picture existence, and then permeating ourselves with what we can only devote ourselves to in free will—to the Christ being: for He stands in earth evolution in a way that allows our connection with Him to be only a free one. [. . .] A spiritual view of the world must unite with a natural, physical world view, and these must unite in the human being, through a free deed. Anyone who wishes to *prove* freedom is still rooted in an ancient, pagan point of view. All proofs of freedom fail; our task is not to prove freedom but grasp hold of it. We take hold of it when we understand the nature of sense-free thinking. Sense-free thinking however needs to establish a connection with the world again; and it does not find this unless it unites with what entered the evolution of the world as new substance through the Mystery of Golgotha.

22. The Grail in the Brain

Extract from a lecture given in The Hague on 25 March 1913

The Grail is also located within each of us, in the castle of the skull, and can nourish our subtlest perceptions in a way that dispels all but the most refined material influence. In a 'small part of the human organism' therefore—and Steiner is referring here to the pineal gland in the brain—is focused the power that can continually rejuvenate and refresh us, however 'wounded' we are by the organism's material processes.

[...] Let's consider what sleep is. The consciousness that permeates the physical and etheric bodies by day is now outside them, and only vegetative processes occur within these bodies; all the forces that were used up during the day are being replenished. We perceive how the forces, especially those consumed in the brain, are renewed from the physical realm. Not that we see the brain as the anatomist would; we see, rather, how we forsake the human being who serves in the physical world as the instrument of consciousness while we are awake. Nevertheless, we clearly understand that this being is our instrument, albeit one that, as it were, lies enchanted within a castle.

Just as the brain resting within the skull may be seen as a symbol, so the human being on earth appears as living enchanted in a castle. The human entity appears as a being surrounded and imprisoned behind stone walls. The symbol of this—the shrivelled symbol as it were—is the skull. Outwardly, it appears in the form of a miniature skull. When we look at the etheric forces that fashion the skull, earthly human beings actually appear to us as beings who find themselves within the skull, imprisoned in this castle. Forces then stream up from the rest of the organism and sustain this being imprisoned in the skull as though in a fortified castle. The forces are directed upwards: first the force comes from the instrument of the human astral body which extends through the human organism. Everything that inspires and lends us strength streams through the nerve fibres. Within us this is all united and appears as a mighty sword we have forged for ourselves on earth. Then the blood's forces stream upwards. Gradually we feel them and begin to recognize them, and they appear to us as what actually wounds the 'brain-being' lying in the enchanted castle of the skull. Like a bleeding lance, the forces stream upwards in the etheric body towards the earthly human being lying within the enchanted castle of the brain; we realize that we can observe everything allowed to flow towards the noblest part of the brain. [. . .]

No matter how much animal-derived food a person may eat, it does not benefit a certain part of the brain, but is simply ballast. Other organs may be nourished by it, but the brain's etheric body immediately rejects all that comes from the animal kingdom. Indeed, from one part of the brain—one small, ennobled part—the etheric body also rejects everything that comes from the plant kingdom, and tolerates only a mineral essence. There, in this vital part of the brain, the mineral essence unites with the purest and noblest radiance entering through the sense organs. Here, the purest, noblest element in light, sound and warmth encounters the most refined products of the mineral kingdom. The noblest part of the brain is nourished by this union between the most delicate sense impressions and the most refined mineral products. The etheric body rejects everything that comes from the plant and animal kingdoms and excludes it from this noblest part of the human brain. [. . .]

This noblest element in the brain is continually sustained through the union of the most delicate sense perceptions and the purest essences of the mineral kingdom. Then, during sleep, when the brain is not thinking, the animal- and plant-derived products formed within the human being flow towards the brain. [. . .] Wounded by the forces in the blood, the human being—whose strength is in thinking—sleeps. The human being must open to nourishment from everything that originates in the kingdoms of nature, and his noblest part must be served by what is most refined. [. . .]

The legend of the Holy Grail tells us of that miraculous food, prepared from the finest effects of the sense impressions and the finest effects of the mineral essences whose purpose is to nourish the noblest part of human beings throughout life on earth. All other nourishment would kill them. This celestial food is contained in the vessel of the Holy Grail.

What occurs otherwise? What forces its way up from the other kingdoms? We find this shown subtly in the original Grail legend: a meal is described where venison is first served. The legend describes this intrusion into the brain, where the Grail eternally hovers—the vessel serving the noblest nourishment of the human being who lies in the castle of the brain, killed by every other form of nourishment. [. . .]

The etheric body works to the extent that it can on the physical body, to rejuvenate and enliven it. It sustains the physical body throughout life, although this physical body is already condemned to death at birth. The etheric body sustains it, as we have seen, by casting out from a small part of the human organism all that derives from the plant and animal kingdoms, retaining only the most refined mineral essence and uniting it with the purest impressions of the external, sensory world.

If we experience this reality deeply enough, we find this noblest part of the human organism revealed in each of us as a copy of the Holy Grail. [. . .]

23. Receiving the Light

Extract from a lecture given in Basel on 1 October 1911

To clairvoyant perception the pineal gland in someone of 'high morality' can appear surrounded by calm light, and is thus reminiscent of the Grail chalice in the Parzival story. In this description of the small, essential organ in the brain, it seems to figure, again, as a meeting place or even doorway where what streams into us from without encounters what rises from within the physical organism. At this moment of encounter, depending on our inner nature and stage of development, this meeting place becomes the locus either of calm confluence or erratic turbulence. It is striking that the quality of 'rays' streaming in to the human being is not simply uniformly 'cosmic' and luminous but is determined by the moral nature of the receiver himself. In other words, we can receive only as much of Christ as we raise ourselves to receive.

The processes that have been described in their more external aspect can also be perceived in us through clairvoyance. When someone stands before us today in a waking state and we observe him through clairvoyant perception, certain rays of light are seen streaming continually from the heart towards the head. Within the head these rays play around the organ known in anatomy as the pineal gland. These streams arise because human blood, a physical substance, is perpetually resolving itself into etheric substance. In the region of the heart there is a continual transformation of the blood into this delicate etheric substance which streams upwards towards the head and glimmers around the pineal gland. This process, the etherization of the blood, can be perceived in us all the time in our waking life.

But during sleep it is different. Then the esoteric observer can see a continual streaming from without into the brain, and also back from the brain to the heart. These streams which ray into us from without in sleep, come from the cosmos, the macrocosm, flowing into the inner constitution of the physical and etheric bodies as they lie in bed. Remarkably, these rays vary greatly in different individuals. Sleeping human beings differ radically from one another; and if those who are a little vain only knew how badly they betray themselves to occult observation when they go to sleep during public gatherings, they would try their level best not to let this happen!

Moral qualities are revealed very clearly in the particular colouring of the streams which flow into human beings during sleep. In an individual of lower moral principles, the streams are quite different from what can be seen in an individual of noble principles. Efforts to dissemble are useless. No dissembling is possible in relation to cosmic forces. The rays streaming into someone who has only a slight inclination towards moral principles, are a brownish-red in colour—various shades tending towards brownish-red. In someone of high moral ideals, the rays are lilac-violet in colour. At the moment of waking or going to sleep a kind of struggle takes place in the region of the pineal gland between what streams down from above and what streams upwards from below. When a person is awake, the intellectual element streams upwards from below in the form of currents of light; and what is of a moral and aesthetic nature streams downwards from above. At the moment of waking or falling asleep, these two currents meet; and in someone who is especially clever but of low morality, a violent struggle between the two streams takes place in the region of the pineal gland. In someone of high morality there is, as it were, a little sea of light around the pineal gland. Moral nobility is revealed when a calm glow surrounds the pineal gland at these moments of falling asleep or waking. In this way a person's moral disposition is reflected in him, and this calm glow of light often extends as far as the heart. Two streams can therefore be perceived in the human being: one macro-cosmic, the other microcosmic. [. . .]

Just as, in the region of the human heart, the blood is continually being transformed into etheric substance, a similar process takes place in the microcosm. We understand this when we turn our minds to the Mystery of Golgotha—to the moment when the blood flowed from the wounds of Jesus Christ.

This blood must not be regarded simply as chemical substance but must be recognized as something altogether unique. When it flowed from His wounds a substance was imparted to our earth which, in uniting with it, constituted an event of the greatest possible significance for all future ages of earth's evolution—and it could happen only once. What came of this blood in the ages that followed? Nothing different from what occurs in the human heart. In the course of earth evolution this blood passes through a process of 'etherization'. And just as our human blood streams upwards from the heart as ether, so since the Mystery of Golgotha the etherized blood of Christ Jesus has been present in the earth's ether. The etheric body of the earth is permeated by the blood—now transformed—which flowed on Golgotha. This is supremely important. If what has thus come to pass through Christ Jesus had not taken place, the human being's condition on earth could only have been as previously described.[30] But since the Mystery of Golgotha it has always been possible for the etheric blood of Christ to flow together with the streams flowing from below upwards within us, from heart to head.

Because the etherized blood of Jesus of Nazareth is present in the etheric body of the earth, it accompanies the etherized human blood streaming upwards from the heart to the brain, so that the human blood stream unites with the blood stream of Christ Jesus. A union of these two streams can, however, only come about if a person can develop true understanding of the Christ impulse. Otherwise there can be no union. The two streams then mutually repel each other, thrust each other away.

VII

INITIATION TODAY: THE TRIALS AND THE QUEST

24. Seeing Heaven in a Wild Flower

Extract from a lecture given in Munich on 6 June 1907

It is interesting that the initiatory quest in human spiritual striving itself furnishes the powers to enhance all levels of the human being right down to the physical organism. The effect of moral, imaginative pictures in meditation works right into the blood's circulation with harmonizing and strengthening effect. At the same time this health-giving impetus we ourselves engender opens us to communion with all other beings.

Only when human beings see the earth as possessing body and soul as a person does, can they have some idea of what Goethe meant when he said 'Everything transitory is but a semblance.' When you see tears run down a human countenance you do not apply the laws of physics to investigate how quickly or how slowly they roll down: they express to you the inner sadness of the soul, just as a smiling face expresses the soul's inner joy. The pupil [of initiation] must educate himself to see in each single flower in the meadow he crosses the outer expression of a living being, the expression of the spirit indwelling the earth. Some flowers seem to be tears, others are the joyful expression of the indwelling earth spirit, its physiognomy that speaks to us. And then everything 'transitory' becomes the 'semblance' of an eternal quality that comes to expression. Feelings like these had to be attained by the disciple of the Grail and by the Rosicrucian. [. . .] What comes to pass in the slow evolution of the human race is something the initiate prefigures. He shows us humanity's evolution in prefiguring pictures, and these pictures work quite differently from the abstract thoughts which the modern materialistic age calls forth. If you picture evolution in such lofty and powerful pictures as the Grail, then the effect is different from that of ordinary knowledge, which cannot exercise any deep influence on your organism. Imaginative knowledge works down on the etheric body and thence on the blood, and this is the medium which acts formatively on the organism. Human beings will become increasingly able to work on their organism through their etheric body. All imaginative knowledge founded on truth is at the same time healing and health-giving: it makes the blood's circulation healthy. Imaginative knowledge is the best educator if we are only strong and devoted enough to allow it to work on us. [...]

Esoteric development is what humanity now needs. Only an earnest, true striving for truth, step by step, will lead to genuine fraternity. This is the 'magician' which can best unite humanity and will serve to bring about the great goal of unity between all. And we shall reach this goal when we seek to do so in the noblest, purest way, hallowing humanity by this means. [...]

25. The Past and Future of the Pineal Gland

Extract from an esoteric lesson given in Munich on 6 June 1907

The pineal gland in the brain, which we have already identified as the 'Grail' in the human organism, is an organ that continues to develop and will become increasingly important in future in relation to our capacity for spiritual perception. In the second extract below, though no mention is made of the pineal gland, Steiner's reference to the 'vessel of gratitude' suggests nevertheless a deep connection.

[...] There was once a time when none of us had eyes. At that time the human being floated and swam in a watery, primeval sea. He had an organ for orientating himself which is present in us now only in a vestigial form. This is the so-called pineal gland, which lies in the upper part of the middle of the head and is somewhat involuted. We can see it in some animals if we remove the top of the skull. This organ enabled the primeval human being to perceive whether he was approaching something helpful or harmful. Above all, though, it was an organ for perceiving warmth and cold. When, in those times, the sun shone down upon earth, the human being could not see it; but the pineal gland led him to the parts of the ocean which it had warmed. And this warmth gave him a feeling of great delight. He would remain there for long periods, drawing very close to the surface so that the rays of the sun could warm him. And because the sun's rays fell directly upon his body, the eyes began to form. Two things were therefore necessary for eyes to develop: the sun had to shine, firstly, but human beings also had to swim to the sun-warmed places and expose themselves to it. If they had not done this but instead had thought 'I will only develop what is already in me', then they might well have developed a larger and larger pineal gland—a monster of an organ—but they would never have received eyes.

We must think about the development of spiritual eyes in the same way. One should not say 'The higher worlds are already within me, I only need to develop them and draw them out of myself'. Primeval human beings were unable to draw the sun out of themselves, but they could form the organs to see it with. We also can only form the organs to see the spiritual sun and the higher worlds: we cannot draw them out of ourselves. And we will never be able to develop these organs if, on the one hand, the spiritual sun does not shine upon us and, on the other, we do not hurry to expose ourselves to it so that it can. The places where the spiritual sun shines for us are the esoteric schools: all who feel drawn to them are warmed by its rays when they heed the instructions and directions they receive there. Every organ which had a past will also have a future. In future, the pineal gland will again become an important organ. People in esoteric schools are already working to form it. The exercises we receive affect not only our astral and etheric bodies but also the pineal gland. When their effect becomes very penetrating it permeates from the pineal gland into the lymph vessels and from there into the blood. All human beings will in the future have a developed pineal gland. [. . .] Those who form their pineal gland in the right way will have a very precious and perfect organ.

Undated extract from advice given on meditation, recorded by Martina von Limburger

The important thing to feel is that, independent of our rational life, something thinks in us of which we can say: not I but *it* thinks in me. Although such thoughts mean little to us at first, we can strengthen and enhance them through a feeling of gratitude to higher powers. If, after each such moment, we say 'I thank you, powers of the higher hierarchies, for letting me perceive this', then these feelings of gratitude and awe allow the moments when higher worlds reveal themselves to increase. We shall be able to hold in memory what at first moved through our soul dim as a dream, and ultimately we shall be able to summon such conditions at will. Then we shall gradually become clear that this thinking in us is always independent of our intellectual thought.

Gratitude is the vessel we lift to the gods so that they may fill it with their wondrous gifts. If, in all earnestness we nurture the feeling of thankfulness then gratitude, loving devotion, must be there to the invisible spiritual givers of life; and the most wonderful way to be led from one's personality to the supersensible is if this guidance passes through gratitude. Gratitude ultimately brings us to veneration and love of the life-bestowing spirit. It gives birth to love, and love opens the heart for the spiritual powers pervading life. If, after every meditation, we rouse in ourselves a sense of gratefulness and reverence—a feeling that we can call a mood of prayer—and are aware what grace we are participating in, we will realize that we are on the right path for worlds of spirit to approach us. [. . .]

26. The Riven Path

Extract from a lecture given in Berlin on 6 May 1909

In the Grail path of initiation, the three soul forces of thinking, feeling and will must first liberate themselves from their interwoven unity in us so that the I or ego can reign ever more consciously over them in sovereign mastery. This sundering process means that we forsake and are forsaken by what previously naturally and unconsciously sustained us—and this can be a very alarming and painful process, leaving us initially plagued by torment and riven by doubt. But as in the Parzival legend, doubt (which both in English and German—'Zweifel'—contains the word 'two' or 'double', suggesting a sundering process) is also a great teacher: the doorway as it were to blessedness.

[...] I have often told you of the great stimulus given to human evolution by the Christ impulse. To understand this, let us think once more of ancient Hebrew consciousness. The ancient Hebrew felt himself one with his 'Fathers'. He said to himself: 'My ego is encompassed by birth and death, but my blood streams into me from my Father Abraham. The blood in my veins is the expression of my ego, of my individuality; it is the blood-stream which flows through the generations and is the expression of my God.'

And so the ancient Hebrew felt himself part of one great whole, secure in the blood-stream which passes down through the generations. Christ says: 'Before Abraham was, I AM'; and 'I and the Father are One.' The human I is linked to a world of spirit by threads which everyone may discover in his own individuality. The Mystery of Golgotha brought to human beings a realization of the I that, without ignoring blood ties, is founded upon itself. [. . .] Therefore people saw in the blood which flowed from the wounds of the Redeemer the expression of the human ego principle, and it was said that 'He who quickens this blood within himself will become a true seer'. But the world was not ripe enough to understand the essence of the Mystery of Golgotha. It was not ripe in the centuries immediately following the coming of Christ, nor is it today. Paul had a vision of the living Christ in the spiritual world; but, after all, who understands those profound Epistles of an initiate? [. . .].

It was only in small circles of initiates that this sacred Christ mystery was preserved. Someone initiated into this mystery experienced the overcoming of the sense-based ego. He experienced this by asking: 'What has been the manner of my life so far? In my quest for truth, I have turned to the things of the outer world. The initiates of the Christ mystery, however, ask me not to wait until external things show me the truth but to seek the invisible in my soul, without stimulus from the external world.'

This quest of the soul for the highest, invisible truth was later called the secret of the Holy Grail. And the Parzival or Grail legend is simply a form of the Christ mystery. The Grail is the holy cup from which Christ drank at the Last Supper and in which Joseph of Arimathea caught the blood as it flowed on Golgotha. The cup was then taken to a holy place and guarded. So long as we do not ask about the invisible, our lot is that of Parzival. Only when he asks, does he become an initiate of the Christ mystery.

Wolfram von Eschenbach speaks in his poem of the three stages through which the human soul passes. The first of these is the stage of outer, material perception. The soul is caught up in matter and allows matter to dictate what is truth. This is the stage of 'stupor' of soul, or 'dullness', as Wolfram von Eschenbach expresses it. And then the soul begins to recognize that the outer world offers only illusion. When the soul perceives that the results of science are not answers but only questions, the stage comes of what Wolfram von Eschenbach calls 'doubt'. From there the soul rises to 'blessedness'—to life in the spiritual worlds.

The Mysteries illumined by the Christ impulse have one quite definite feature in common which raises them to a higher level than that of the more ancient, pre-Christian mysteries. Initiation always means that we attain a higher kind of vision, and that our soul undergoes higher development. Before we set out on this path, three faculties live within the soul: thinking, feeling and will. We have these three soul-powers innate in us. In ordinary life in the modern world, these three soul-powers are intimately intertwined. The human ego is interwoven with thinking, feeling and will because, before someone attains initiation, he has not worked with the powers of the ego to develop his higher members. [. . .]

In true initiation it is as if a person's organization is divided into three parts, with the I reigning as king over the three. Whereas in ordinary circumstances the spheres of thinking, feeling and will are not clearly separated, when we set out on the path of higher development thoughts begin to arise in us which are not immediately tinged with feeling, but are permeated with the element of sympathy or antipathy according to the free choice of the I. Feeling does not immediately attach itself to a thought, but a person divides instead, as it were, into three: a person of feeling, a person of thinking, a person of will; and the I, as king, rules over these three. At a definite stage of initiation he is, in this sense, divided in three. [. . .] Someone who is not able or ripe enough to bear this separation of his being will not attain the fruits of initiation. The sufferings that crowd upon him in his immature state will keep him back. A person who approaches the Holy Grail but is not worthy, will suffer as Amfortas suffered. He can only be redeemed by one who brings the forces of good. He is freed from his sufferings by Parzival.

And now let us return once more to what initiation brings about. The seeking soul finds the spiritual world; the soul finds the Holy Grail which has now become the symbol of the spiritual world. Individual initiates have experienced this. They have gone the way of Parzival, becoming like kings looking down on the three bodies, astral, etheric and physical. The initiate says to himself: 'I am king over my purified astral body which can only be purified when I strive to emulate Christ.' He must not hold to any outer reference point, to anything in the external world, but unite in the innermost depths of his soul with the Christ principle. Everything that binds him with the world of sense must fall away in that supreme moment. Lohengrin represents such an initiate. In the legend, one may not ask his name or rank: in other words, what connects him with the external sense-world. Someone devoid of both name and rank, is called 'homeless', and is pervaded by the Christ principle. He likewise looks down on the etheric body, which has become life spirit,[31] as upon something that is now separate from the astral body. This etheric body bears him upwards to higher worlds, where the laws of space and time do not hold sway. The symbol of this etheric body and its organs is the swan who bears Lohengrin over the sea in a boat (the physical body), over the material world. The physical body is felt to be an instrument.

The soul on earth who experiences a new impulse through initiation is symbolized in the figure of Elsa von Brabant. This shows us that the Lohengrin legend is among many other things a portrayal of initiation in the mysteries associated with the Holy Grail. Thus in the eleventh to the thirteenth centuries, these secrets of the Holy Grail were taught in connection with the Christ mystery. The knights of the Grail were Christian initiates. [. . .]

The world and 'all it contains' is born out of the spirit; we are born, and called to rise to the spirit. Spiritual science shows us that the spirit lies exhausted in matter, that physical substance is the magic robe of the spiritual realm. Living as we do in the material world, it is our task to charm the spirit out of this magic robe. The spiritual finds its resurrection in the human being, in the human soul that rises above itself. [. . .]

27. The Parzival Saga as Modern Initiation

Extracts from various chapters in *Knowledge of the Higher Worlds,* 8th edition, 1918

Although there is no mention of Parzival or the Grail in the passages below, these excerpts from Steiner's seminal work on self-development are certainly in tune with and correspond to much that has so far surfaced. The Grail path as one of modern initiation in the midst of everyday life, and its invisibility and inaudibility next to the stridency and cacophony of much of that life, make such a path of quiet perseverance all the more essential today. Below I have juxtaposed passages from Knowledge of the Higher Worlds *with small tableaux from the Parzival story that seem to illustrate some of the 'trials' which Steiner describes. While some of the stages of higher knowledge referred to here may seem beyond the ken of many if not most readers, including myself, Steiner invariably also roots these stages of initiation in common daily experiences which all of us undergo, and which he says are a real and firm foundation for further self-development. In other words, whether we are aware of it or not, we have all already started out on a quest.*

Initiation

We can only fathom the mysteries of existence as far as our own degree of maturity allows. For this reason alone the path to the higher stages of knowledge and power is beset with obstacles. A firearm should not be used until sufficient experience has been gained to avoid disaster caused by its use. A person initiated today without further ado would lack the experience he would gain during his future incarnations, when he could achieve higher knowledge in the normal course of his development. At the portal of initiation, therefore, this experience must be supplied in some other way. Thus the first instructions given to the pupil for initiation serve as a substitute for these future experiences. These are the so-called trials he has to undergo; they are in fact a normal consequence of the life of soul when exercises such as those described in previous chapters are pursued in the right way. [...]

The would-be initiate must come into contact with certain things and facts belonging to the higher worlds, but he can only see and hear them if his feeling is ripe for the perception of the spiritual forms, colours and tones described in the chapters on Preparation and Enlightenment.[32]

The trial by fire

The first trial consists in obtaining a truer vision than the average person has of the corporeal attributes of lifeless things, and then of plants, animals and human beings. This does not mean what at present is called scientific knowledge, for it is a question not of science but of vision. As a rule, the would-be initiate proceeds to learn how the objects of nature and the beings gifted with life reveal themselves to the spiritual ear and the spiritual eye. In a certain way these things then lie disclosed—naked—before the beholder. The qualities which can then be seen and heard are hidden from physical eyes and ears. For physical perception they are concealed as if by a veil. The falling away of this veil for the would-be initiate involves a process known as 'spiritual burning away'. The first trial is therefore known as the trial by fire.

For many people, ordinary life is itself a more or less unconscious process of initiation through the fire trial. Such people have passed through a wealth of experience, so that their self-confidence, courage and fortitude have been greatly strengthened in a normal manner while learning to bear sorrow, disappointment and failure in their undertakings with greatness of soul, and especially with equanimity and unbroken strength. Thus they are often initiates without knowing it, and little is then needed to unseal their spiritual hearing and sight so that they become clairvoyant. It must be noted that a genuine fire-trial is not intended to satisfy the pupil's curiosity. It is true that he learns of many remarkable things of which others can have no inkling, yet this acquisition of knowledge is not the end, but the means to the end; the end consists in the attainment, thanks to this knowledge of the higher worlds, of greater and truer self-confidence, enhanced courage, and a magnanimity and perseverance quite different from anything that can generally be acquired in the lower world.

Having left his mother, yet still naively following her instructions to the letter—with no knowledge at all of the world—Parzival has gone on his headstrong way and done some harm in the process, frequently breaking the code of knightly conduct. This seems reminiscent of Steiner's words above about the 'firearm' that can do damage. Parzival is somewhat 'trigger-happy' in his initial, disastrous exploits. Arriving at the castle of Gurnemanz, the latter sees his beauty and promise and takes him under his wing, giving him a set of moral precepts to follow and hoping that he will marry his daughter Liaze. Refusing to stay there, though, Parzival still feels he must accomplish greater deeds. The moral precepts of Gurnemanz, though laudable, are imposed on him from without and not yet his own inner possession. Indeed, one of them—to ask few questions—will lead him seriously astray when he arrives at the Grail castle. But Parzival has already started to break away from such externally imposed authority, as expressed metaphorically by his riding away from Gurnemanz to seek greater deeds and so become worthier of whatever destiny holds in store.

On this quest he arrives at the besieged city of Pelrapeire, which is separated from its attackers by a deep gorge crossed only by a wicker bridge. The defending knights let out a tumult of shouts to scare off Parzival as he approaches, and the bridge sways perilously; but undeterred Parzival leads his horse fearlessly across the abyss. The defending knights retreat inside the citadel at the sight of him and bar its gates. But he knocks, offers his services and is admitted by Queen Condwiramur, whom the besieging army wishes to compel, against her will, to marry its leader King Clamide. Parzival gains entry and welcome where mere force has failed.

In these brief images one can see the 'crossing' to a different kind of perception, requiring 'courage and fortitude'. The citadel of Condwiramur is a spiritual location which cannot be stormed by outward compulsion. Steiner speaks above also of 'magnanimity' and it is striking that on entering the citadel Parzival's character seems to undergo a change from impetuosity to generosity: there is little food in the besieged city, but Parzival makes sure that the splendid meal prepared for him is instead shared out amongst the people.

The occult script

The pupil may always turn back after the trial by fire. He will then resume his life, strengthened in body and soul, and wait for a future incarnation to continue his initiation. In his present incarnation he will prove himself a more useful member of society and of humanity than he was before. In whatever position he may find himself, his steadiness, circumspection, resolve and benevolent influence over his fellow human beings will have greatly increased.

But if, after completing the trial by fire he should wish to continue the path, a certain script generally adopted in esoteric training must now be revealed to him. The true esoteric teachings reveal themselves in this script, because the hidden (occult) qualities of things can neither be expressed in ordinary language nor in ordinary writing. The pupils of the initiates translate the teachings into ordinary language as best they can. The occult script reveals itself to the soul when the latter has attained spiritual perception, for it is inscribed enduringly in the spiritual world. It cannot be learned as artificial writing is learned and read. The pupil grows into clairvoyant knowledge in an appropriate way, and during this growth a new strength is developed in his soul, as a new faculty, through which he feels himself impelled to decipher the occurrences and the beings of the spiritual world as he would decipher the characters of a script. This strength, with the experience it brings of the corresponding trial, might possibly awaken in the soul as though of its own accord as the soul continually develops, but following the guidance of experienced spiritual investigators skilled in deciphering the occult script, is a surer path.

The signs of the occult script are not arbitrarily invented; they correspond to the forces actively working in the world. They teach us the language of things. It becomes immediately apparent to the pupil that the signs he is now learning correspond to the forms, colours, and tones which he learned to perceive during his preparation and enlightenment. He realizes that all he learned previously was only like learning to spell, and that he is only now beginning to read in the higher worlds. All the separate shapes, tones and colours reveal themselves to him now in one great connected whole. Now for the first time he attains complete certainty in observing the higher worlds. Hitherto he could never know positively whether the things he saw were rightly seen. A systematic understanding is now also at last possible between the pupil and the initiate in the spheres of higher knowledge. For whatever form the association between an initiate and another person may take in ordinary life, higher knowledge in its immediate form can only be imparted by the initiate in the sign-language described here.

Thanks to this language the student also learns certain rules of conduct and certain duties of which he formerly knew nothing. Having learned these he is able to perform actions endowed with a significance and a meaning that the actions of one not initiated can never possess. He acts out of the higher worlds. Guidance relating to such action can only be read and understood in terms of the occult script.

Yet it must be emphasized that there are people unconsciously gifted with the ability and faculty to perform such actions, though they have never undergone esoteric training. Such helpers of the world and of humanity pass through life bestowing blessings and performing good deeds. For reasons discussed here, gifts have been bestowed on them which appear supernatural. What distinguishes them from the pupil for initiation is only that the latter acts consciously and with full insight into the whole situation. He acquires by training the gifts bestowed on others by higher powers for the good of humanity. We can sincerely revere these favoured of God;

but we should not therefore dismiss the work of esoteric training as superfluous.

After being admitted to Condwiramur's citadel, Parzival goes to sleep in a bed surrounded by candles 'as if for a funeral'. In the middle of the night, Queen Condwiramur comes to his bedside like an apparition of beauty. She kneels beside him and 'bends over his face', weeping in sorrow and hope for her people. At this Parzival awakens. Queen Condwiramur offers to lie with him, but Parzival refuses, saying this would not be fitting. He only agrees provided their bodies do not touch: and thus they lie side by side as if with a 'sword of purity' between them. Lying there, Condwiramur tells Parzival of her hopes that he will liberate her from the army of King Clamide. Before the sun rises the next day, she slips away. Parzival fights off and defeats the besiegers and frees the citadel. Condwiramur gladly receives Parzival as her husband; but they only withdraw the 'sword of purity' and consummate their marriage after the third night.

If we take the citadel of Condwiramur as at least an outpost of spiritualized perception, and Condwiramur herself as a metaphor for his increasing intimacy with the connected whole of a spiritual world, some correspondences can be found here with Steiner's words about the occult script. The ritual intention in the candles surrounding Parzival's bed convey his entry into a realm from which arbitrariness is banished. The mention of a funeral might hint at the need to die away from ordinary, sensory existence into a new realm, and it is interesting that this scene takes place at night, when one can be more open and 'awake' to the world of spirit. The image of Condwiramur bending over Parzival so that they meet face to face when Parzival awakens, suggests this awakening to a higher reality. At the same time there is an immediate emphasis in the story on rules of conduct and propriety—now no longer imposed but emerging from within Parzival himself. This shows Parzival's increasing discernment and capacity to 'act out of the higher will'.

On the other hand, as is soon to become apparent, his initial success in this trial is mirrored by his subsequent grave failure to ask the redeeming question at the Grail castle. It is quite possible that any progress we make in self-development takes a long time to become fully integrated and consistently reliable in the psyche. In failing to ask that essential question, Parzival shows he is still, to some extent at least, allowing external precepts to govern him.

The trial by water

Once the student has learned the sign-script, another trial awaits him. This is to show whether he can move with freedom and assurance in the higher worlds. In ordinary life he is impelled to action by external motives. He works at some occupation because one duty or another is imposed on him by circumstances. It need hardly be mentioned that the student must in no way neglect any of his duties in ordinary life because he is engaged in higher worlds. No duty in a higher world can force us to neglect a single duty in the ordinary world. The father will remain just as good a father to his family, the mother just as good a mother, and neither an official, soldier nor anyone else will be diverted from his work by becoming an esoteric student. On the contrary, all the qualities which make a human being capable and effective are enhanced in the student to a degree incomprehensible to the uninitiated. If, in the eyes of the uninitiated, this does not always appear to be the case, it is simply because they often lack the ability to judge the initiate correctly. The deeds of the latter are not always intelligible to the former. But this too is only noticeable in certain instances.

At this stage of initiation there are duties which arise from no external stimulus. The pupil will not be moved to action by external pressures or circumstances, but only through adherence to the rules of conduct revealed to him in the occult script. He must now show in this second 'trial' that, guided by such a rule, his actions can have the same reliability with which, for instance, an official performs his duties. For this purpose, and in the course of his further training, he will find himself faced by a specific task. He must perform some action resulting from observations based on what he has learned during preparation and enlightenment. And he must recognize what he has to do through the understanding he has acquired of the occult script. If he recognizes his duty and acts rightly, he has been successful in this trial. Success can be recognized in the alteration produced by his action in the forms, colours and tones perceived by his spiritual eyes and ears. Exact indications are given, as the training progresses, showing how these forms appear and are experienced after the action has been performed, and the pupil must know how to produce this change. This trial is known as the trial by water, because in his activity in these higher worlds the pupil is deprived of any support from outward circumstances, just as a swimmer moves through water in which he is out of his depth. This activity must be repeated until the pupil attains absolute poise and assurance.

This trial, too, involves acquiring a certain quality. Through his experiences in the higher worlds, the pupil develops this quality in a short time to such a high degree that he would otherwise have to go through many incarnations, in the ordinary course of his development, before he could acquire it to the same extent. The essential thing is that he must be guided only by the results of his higher perception and reading of the occult script, in order to produce the changes in question in these higher regions of existence. If, in the course of his activity, he should introduce any of his own opinions and desires, or should he diverge for one moment from the laws which he has recognized to be right, in order to follow his own wilful inclinations, then the result would be altogether different from what should properly come about. He would lose sight of the goal to which his action tended, and confusion would result. Hence ample opportunity is given him in the course of this trial to develop self-control. And that is what matters above all. Here again, people can more easily succeed in this trial if their previous life has led them to acquire self-control. Whoever has acquired the capacity to pursue high principles and ideals, while putting into the background all personal predilections, whoever is capable of always performing his duty when inclinations and sympathies are only too ready to divert him from it, is unconsciously already an initiate in the midst of ordinary life. It will not take much for him to succeed in this particular trial. Indeed, a certain measure of initiation unconsciously acquired in life will, as a rule, be indispensable for success in this second trial. For just as it is difficult for those who have not learned to spell correctly in their childhood to make good this deficiency when they have grown up, so it is difficult to develop the necessary degree of self-control at the moment of looking into the higher worlds if this ability has not been acquired to a certain degree in ordinary life. The objects of the physical world do not alter, whatever the nature of our wishes, desires, and inclinations. In the higher worlds, however, our wishes, desires, and inclinations are causes that produce effects. If we wish to produce a particular effect in these worlds, we must strictly follow the right rules and subdue every arbitrary impulse.

One human quality is of very special importance at this stage of initiation: an absolutely healthy and reliable faculty of judgement. Attention should be paid to the training of this faculty during all the previous stages; and this will show whether the pupil is equipped for the true path of knowledge. Further progress is now only possible if he can distinguish illusion, superstition, and every kind of phantasmagoria from true reality. This is at first more difficult to accomplish at the higher stages of existence than in the lower. Every prejudice, every cherished opinion with regard to the things in question, must vanish; truth alone must guide us. There must be perfect readiness to abandon any idea, opinion, or inclination directly logical thought demands it. Certainty in higher worlds is only to be attained when one does not cherish personal opinion.

Individuals whose mode of thinking tends to fancifulness and superstition can make no progress on the path to higher knowledge. It is a precious treasure that the student is to acquire. He rids himself of all doubt about higher worlds. They reveal themselves to his gaze in their full lawfulness. But he cannot acquire this treasure so long as he is the prey of fancies and illusions. If his imagination and his prejudices ran away with his intellect this would be very bad for him. Dreamers and fancy-ridden people are as unfit for the path to higher knowledge as those swayed by superstitions. This cannot be overemphasized, for the most dangerous enemies on the way to knowledge of the higher worlds lurk in fantastical reveries and superstitions. Yet no one need believe that the student loses all sense of poetry in life, all power of enthusiasm because the words: 'You must rid yourself of all prejudice' are inscribed above the portal leading to the second trial of initiation, and because the portal to the first trial bears the words: 'Without healthy human reason all your efforts are in vain.'

After his failure and unreadiness at the Grail castle, Parzival continues on his way, and encounters the lady Jeschute whom he had so disgraced in his more wilful days. He realizes the consequences of his misdeeds and, through a further battle, reunites her with her husband and redeems his harmful error. Together they visit a nearby hermit's cave where Parzival swears an oath on a holy casket he finds there, claims full responsibility for his former foolish actions and expresses his profound regret. Jeschute's honour is fully restored.

In other words, Parzival 'performs some action resulting from what he has learned ... and recognizes his duty'. No outward circumstances compel him to this action. He shows self-control and a capacity to distance himself enough from his former desires to acknowledge higher laws. He shows judgement and discernment.

So often though, one scene of success in the epic is mirrored by another in which it becomes clear that Parzival still has far to go. Shortly after this episode, Parzival finds himself wandering alone at Whitsun, with outward fame and inwardly unfulfilled. Though it is May the ground is, somewhat strangely, lightly dusted with snow. Parzival sees a goose being chased by a hawk, which pierces it so that three drops of blood fall on the snow. Gazing at these three drops Parzival falls into a dream-like trance, beholding there the image of his beloved Condwiramur. He is so 'far gone' in this fantasy that he scarcely perceives the knights who come to battle with him as he sits there, just waking up briefly to unseat them from their horses then falling back into his deep reverie. It is not until Gawain covers the three drops of blood with a scarf that

Parzival wakes up to reality again and is surprised to find his lance has been broken in combat.

Through his preparation, Parzival has acquired the capacity to do the right thing (defeat his combatants) by deep instinct and by virtue of the power of the sleeping will. Nevertheless this scene, even though it brings Parzival a vision of his true love, also suggests something of what Steiner calls 'fancies and illusions' above. Perhaps because he is not yet inwardly fulfilled by an essential connection with the Whitsun event, with the deed of Christ as inner experience, his outer surroundings have an unseasonally chilly feel, as expressed in the dusting of snow, and his gaze is fettered by the sensory blood of the 'goose': the same name he himself was called in mockery and insult when he was expelled from the Grail castle.

The trial by air

Once advanced sufficiently in this way, a third trial awaits the pupil. Here he finds no definite goal to be reached. All is left in his own hands. He finds himself in a situation where nothing impels him to act. He must find his way alone, everything is left in his own hands. No things or people are there to stimulate him to action. Nothing and nobody can give him the strength he needs except himself alone. Failure to find this inner strength will leave him standing where he was. Few of those, however, who have successfully passed the previous trials will fail to find the necessary strength at this point. Either they will have turned back before or they succeed here also. All that the pupil needs is the capacity to come to terms with his own nature swiftly, for here he must find his higher self in the truest sense of the word. He must instantly decide to listen to the promptings of the spirit in all things, without doubt or hesitation. Any hesitation would show he was still unfit. Whatever prevents him from listening to the voice of the spirit must be boldly overcome. Presence of mind is required here, and training at this stage is concerned with the perfect development of this quality. All inducements to act or even to think which the pupil has previously been used to, now cease. In order not to remain inactive he must not lose himself, for only within himself can he find the single firm point where he can gain a firm hold. No one on reading this, without further acquaintance with these matters, should feel an antipathy for this principle of being thrown back on oneself, for success in this trial brings with it a moment of supreme happiness.

At this stage, no less than at the others, ordinary life is itself an esoteric training for many. Life itself has been a training in this sense for anyone who has reached the point of being able, when suddenly confronted with some task or problem in life, to make a swift decision without hesitation or delay: situations in which success is instantly forfeit if immediate action is not taken. Someone quick to act to avoid imminent misfortune, who has turned this ability into a permanent personal quality, has unconsciously acquired the degree of maturity necessary for the third trial. At this stage everything depends on the development of absolute presence of mind. This trial is known as the trial by air, because the pupil undergoing it can depend neither on external incentive nor on the forms, tones, and colours which he has learned at the stages of preparation and enlightenment. The only thing he can rely on is himself.

After Parzival's 'fancy-ridden' vision with the three drops of blood, he is celebrated and acclaimed at King Arthur's court. The Grail messenger Kundry enters and publicly casts scorn on Par-

zival, accusing him of failure at the Grail castle—which was, as we have seen, ultimately a failure of compassion. Kundry piles on the insults and humiliates Parzival in the midst of his worldly renown, giving him a deep sense of shame—which is of course closely connected with the psyche's sense of deepening conscience—and enabling him to hearken more keenly to the promptings of his spirit. Though he is humiliated, this shame also acts as a spur to him to make himself worthy of the Grail. Following this episode Parzival disappears almost altogether from the epic while the focus shifts to Gawain. It is as if a deep inner process is underway, over which a veil must be drawn, during which significant changes are slowly unfolding. We hear that Parzival's sword is shattered in battle but is made whole again in the magic spring of Karnant, which suggests a radical reconfiguration of the soul's power. During his wanderings, he returns to the hermit's cave and re-encounters the leitmotif of Sigune holding her dead bridegroom, to which Steiner refers on page [37]. The cave seems to figure in the epic as a place of deep inner reflection and access to spiritual realities, and once again we sense that Parzival is drawing close to the Grail castle. After leaving Sigune, Parzival meets a Grail knight who charges him. Parzival unseats his combatant but at the same time his own horse plunges down a ravine. He himself barely escapes the same fate by grabbing hold of an overhanging branch. In other words, with great presence of mind, he 'finds the single firm point where he can gain a sure hold' and 'acts to avoid imminent misfortune'. Taking the Grail knight's horse he finds himself eventually—again—at the cave, in the presence once more of the hermit Trevrizent. It seems significant that he is now carried by a Grail horse, as a deep impulse of will which finds its true direction unswervingly. Trevrizent now gives him a panoramic overview of earthly evolution and at last a real understanding of the deed of Christ and its significance. He also explains the meaning of the Grail to him. Parzival stays in the cave for 15 days, meditating in great simplicity during this, the last preparatory stage of his initiation, and then assumes 'full responsibility for his destiny', thus coming to rely exclusively on himself. After this—having in other words listened deeply to what Steiner here calls the 'voice of the spirit'—he is free to continue on his journey.

The temple of higher wisdom

By successfully passing this trial the pupil may enter the temple of higher wisdom. Very little more—only the barest indication—can be said about this. The task now to be performed is often expressed by saying that the pupil must take an oath never to betray anything he has learned. These expressions, however, 'oath' and 'betray', are inappropriate and actually misleading. There is no question of an oath in the ordinary sense of the word, but rather of something learned by experience at this stage of development. The pupil learns how to apply higher knowledge, how to place it at the service of humanity. He begins to truly understand the world. It is not so much a question of withholding higher truths from others, but far more of serving them in the right way and with the necessary tact. The 'silence' he learns to keep is a quite different matter. He acquires this fine quality with regard to things he had previously spoken, and especially with regard to the way in which they were spoken. He would be a poor initiate who did not place all the higher knowledge he had acquired at the service of humanity, as well and as far as possible. The only obstacle to communication about these matters is the lack of understanding from a recipient. It is true, of course, that higher knowledge does not lend itself to casual talk; but no one having reached the stage of development described above is actually forbidden from saying anything. No other person, no being imposes an oath on him with this intent. Everything is left to his own responsibility, and he learns in every situation to discover within himself what he has to do; and the oath means only that he is fit to bear this responsibility. [. . .]

[The pupil] acquires the capacity to retain knowledge of the higher truths ever present in his soul. Ordinary memory would be unequal to this task. We must unite and become one with the higher truths. We must not only know them, but be able, quite as a matter of course, to apply them in living actions, just as we normally eat and drink. They must become our practice, our habit, our inclination. There must be no need to keep thinking about them in the ordinary sense; they must come to living expression through the human being himself; they must flow through us as the currents of life flow through our organism. In this way we will raise ourselves increasingly, in a spiritual sense, to the level to which nature has physically raised us.

In the subsequent story of Parzival, he has two further significant battles with knights whom he does not initially recognize but who turn out to be Gawain, his comrade in arms, and Feirefiz, his half-brother. Only after fighting each other do they perceive each other's real nature and name. We will return to this strand of the story a little later ('Division of the personality'). Following the resolution of these combats, and the conscious reunion of these three major figures in the epic, Kundry comes again as messenger to lead Parzival to the Grail castle, for his name now shines from the chalice as its new king. On arriving at the castle, he has finally endured and matured enough to ask the critical, compassionate question, 'Uncle, what ails you?', thus bringing redemption to the suffering Amfortas.

Here Parzival 'unites and becomes one' with the higher truths and places his compassionate knowledge at humanity's service, as embodied in the ailing Amfortas. In witnessing the Grail ritual again, Parzival is, one can say, engaging fully in an 'oath' in the sense Steiner describes it here. The idea that one applies higher truths in living actions, 'just as we normally eat and drink' is reminiscent of the Grail as a source of nourishment and healing, from which 'currents of life flow'.

Chakra development

This next passage from Knowledge of the Higher Worlds *picks up on the theme of 'life currents' above. Recalling Steiner's references to the pineal gland in the brain as the Grail of the human organism which mediates the influx of spirit, we can see a relevance to our theme in the establishing of the 'centre' in the head. This later extends and descends to the larynx—and here we can also remember Steiner's vision of the future human capacity to 'create through the word'—and ultimately to the heart. The word 'beatitude' in this passage is very close to and possibly synonymous with the medieval term 'Saelde' (see page [144]) as the ultimate goal of Parzival's journey from dullness through doubt to bliss and blessedness.*

If the pupil follows the directions that have been given him, he introduces into his etheric body currents and movements which are in harmony with the laws and the evolution of the world to which he belongs. Consequently these instructions are reflections of the great laws of cosmic evolution. They consist of the above-mentioned and similar exercises in meditation and concentration which, if correctly practised, produce the results described. The student must at certain times let these instructions permeate his soul with their content, so that he is inwardly entirely filled with it. A simple start is made with a view to the deepening of the logical activity of the mind and the producing of an inward intensification of thought. Thought is thereby made free and independent of all sense impressions and experiences; it is concentrated in one point which is held entirely under control. Thus a preliminary centre is formed for the currents of the etheric body. This centre is not yet in the region of the heart but in the head, and it appears to the clairvoyant as the point of departure for movements and currents. No esoteric training can be successful which does not first create this centre. If the latter were first formed in the region of the heart the aspiring clairvoyant would doubtless obtain glimpses of higher worlds, but would lack all true insight into the connection between these higher worlds and the world of our senses. This, however, is an unconditional necessity for the human being at his present stage of evolution. The clairvoyant must not become a visionary; he must retain a firm footing upon the earth.

The centre in the head, once duly established, is then transferred lower down, to the region of the larynx. This is achieved by further exercises in concentration. Then the currents of the etheric body radiate from this point and illumine the astral space surrounding the individual.

Continued practice enables the pupil to govern the position of this etheric body himself. Hitherto this position depended upon external forces proceeding from the physical body. Through further development the student is able to direct his etheric body as he wishes. This faculty is achieved by currents moving approximately along both hands and centred in the two-petalled lotus in the region of the eyes. All this is made possible through the radiations from the larynx assuming round forms, of which a number flow to the two-petalled lotus and thence form undulating currents along the hands. As a further development, these currents branch out and ramify in the most delicate manner and become, as it were, a kind of web which encompasses the entire etheric body as though with a membrane or network. Whereas the etheric body was not previously closed off from the outer world, so that the life currents from the universal ocean of life flowed freely in and out of it, these currents now have to pass through this membrane. Thus the individual becomes sensitive to these external streams; they become perceptible to him.

And now comes the time to give the complete system of currents and movements its centre situated in the region of the heart. This again is achieved by persevering with the exercises in concentration and meditation; and at this point also the stage is reached when the pupil can hear the inner word. All things now acquire a new significance for him. They become as it were spiritually audible in their inmost nature, and speak to him of their essential being. The currents described above place him in touch with the inner being of the world to which he belongs. He begins to participate inwardly in the life of his environment and can let it reverberate in the movements of his lotus flowers.

At this point the spiritual world is entered. If the pupil has advanced so far, he acquires a new understanding of all that the great teachers of humanity have uttered. The sayings of the Buddha and the Gospels, for instance, produce a new effect on him. They pervade him with a sense of beatitude of which he previously had no inkling. The ring of their words accords with the movements and rhythms he has now developed within himself. He can now have direct knowledge that a being such as Buddha or the writers of the Gospels did not give utterance to their personal revelations but to those which flowed into them from the inmost essence of things. [. . .]

The individual frees himself from everything which depends only upon the faculties of his own personal nature. He ceases to view things from his own separate standpoint; and the boundaries fettering him to his circumscribed self disappear. The secrets of the spiritual world reveal themselves to his inner self. This is liberation. For those fetters constrain the individual to regard things and beings according to his personal idiosyncrasies. And it is from this personal manner of seeing things that the pupil must free himself.

Division of the personality

Above we saw how Parzival meets and fights with Gawain and Feirefiz before fully and consciously recognizing and perceiving them. Though there is no scope here to illustrate it, these three major figures in the epic embody particular qualities and characteristics that suggest each is emblematic of a distinct power of the soul: Parzival, the one who 'pierces' through things with the linearity of thinking*; Gawain, whose warmth of heart and also his battles with, for instance, a 'terrifying beast, a lion the size of a horse' identify him with* feeling *and the astral domain; and Feirefiz, whose enormous strength, and command of a 'vast army' seem expressive of the* will. *Below Steiner describes how the threads* *between the three soul forces are severed during higher development, and must be reunited consciously. The Parzival epic 'individualizes' them as separate figures, then reunites them very shortly before the Grail is finally attained.*

[...] Great changes take place in the pupil's finer bodies, as described above. These changes are connected with certain processes in the development of the three fundamental forces of the soul: will, feeling and thinking. Before esoteric training, these forces are connected in a way ordained by higher cosmic laws. Our will, feeling and thinking are not arbitrary. A particular idea arising in the mind is naturally attended by a particular feeling; or it leads to a resolve of the will in an equally natural manner. We enter a room, find it stuffy, and open the window. We hear our name called and hearken. We are questioned and we answer. We perceive an ill-smelling object and experience a feeling of disgust. These are simple connections between thinking, feeling, and will. When we survey human life we find that everything is founded on such interconnections. Indeed, our life is not thought 'normal' unless such a connection, founded on the laws of human nature, is observed between thinking, feeling and will. It would be thought contrary to these laws if the sight of an ill-smelling object gave anyone pleasure, or if anyone, on being questioned, did not answer. The success anticipated from a right kind of upbringing or education is based on the assumption that a connection between thinking, feeling and will can be established in a child in conformity with human nature. Certain ideas are conveyed to him on the assumption that they will be associated, in regular fashion, with his feelings or will activity.

[...] In the course of higher development, the threads connecting the three fundamental forces are severed. At first this severance occurs only within the finer soul organism, but at a still higher stage the separation extends also to the physical body. It is a fact that in higher spiritual development the brain divides into three separate parts. This separation is not physically perceptible in the ordinary way, nor can it be demonstrated by the most sensitive instruments. Yet it occurs, and the clairvoyant has means of observing it. The brain of the higher clairvoyant divides into three independently active entities: the thought-brain, feeling-brain, and will-brain.

Thus the organs of thinking, feeling, and will become individualized; their connection is no longer maintained by laws inherent in them, but must be managed by the individual's own awakened higher consciousness. This, then, is the change which the pupil observes in himself: that no connection arises of itself between an idea and a feeling or a will impulse, unless he himself provides one. No impulse urges him from thought to action unless he himself gives rise to this impulse in freedom. From then on he can confront a fact which before his training would have filled him with glowing love or bitter hatred, with no feeling response; and he can remain impassive at the thought which formerly would have spurred him to action, as though of its own accord. Through resolves of his will he can perform actions which no one who has not undergone esoteric training can see the slightest reason for. The pupil's great achievement is to attain complete mastery over the combined activity of the three soul forces; and at the same time, responsibility for this activity is placed entirely in his own hands.

The Greater Guardian

According to Steiner, and described below, following this division of and conscious regaining of mastery over the forces of the soul, the initiate encounters a luminous figure of light. Though this figure is not further identified here, its luminosity and love, its concern for the ultimate redemption not just of the individual but of all humanity, certainly suggest it to be Christ. Here, then, as at the end of the Parzival epic—in the uniting of pagan and Christian through the figure of 'black-and-white' Feirefiz, who marries the Grail queen and spreads the Grail message across the globe—we have a sense of the ultimate future reunion of all humanity with itself, and with its highest exemplar and ideal.

When the pupil has recognized all the elements from which he must liberate himself, a sublime being of light stands before him whose beauty is difficult to describe in human language. This encounter takes place when the sundering of the organs of thinking, feeling and will extend to the physical body, so that their reciprocal connection is no longer regulated by themselves but by higher consciousness, which has now entirely liberated itself from physical conditions. The organs of thinking, feeling and will, have then become instruments under the sway of the human soul, which exercises its dominion over them from supersensible regions. The soul, thus liberated from all bonds of the senses, is now confronted by the second Guardian of the Threshold who speaks somewhat as follows:

> *You have released yourself from the world of the senses. You have your rightful place in the supersensible world. You can now work out of this world. For your own sake, you no longer*

require your physical body in its present form. If your intention were merely to acquire the faculties necessary for life in the supersensible world, you no longer need return to the sense world. But now, gaze on me. See how immeasurably I am raised above all that you have made of yourself up to now. You have attained your present degree of perfection through the faculties you were able to develop in the sense world as long as you were still dependent on it. But now an era must begin for you when your liberated powers will work further in the world of the senses. So far you have only achieved self-realization; but now, having become free yourself, you can liberate all your companions in the sense world. Until now you have striven as an individual; now make yourself a member of the whole so that you bring into the supersensible world not yourself alone but everything else that exists in the world of the senses. You will some day be able to unite with me, but I cannot find blessedness as long as others are still unredeemed! As a liberated individual you could enter immediately into the supersensible spheres, but then you would be obliged to gaze down upon all the unredeemed beings in the sense world. You would have separated your destiny from theirs. But you are all interconnected; you all had to descend into the sense world in order to gather from it powers needed for the higher world. If you separate yourself from the others you will misuse the powers you have been able to develop only in association with them. If they had not descended, then nor could you have done so; without them the powers needed for your supersensible existence would be lacking. You must now share with the others the powers you acquired in their company. I therefore forbid you admission into the highest regions of the supersensible world as long as you have not applied the powers you have acquired to the

> *redemption of the world to which you belong. With the powers you have already achieved you may sojourn in the lower regions of the supersensible world; but before the portal of the higher spheres I stand (as the Cherubim with fiery sword at the gates of paradise) and I forbid you to enter as long as you retain powers that have not been put to use in the sense world. And if you will not apply your powers in this way, others coming after you will. Then a higher supersensible world will receive all the fruits of the sense world, but the ground in which you were rooted will be withdrawn from you. [...]*

An indescribable splendour radiates from the second Guardian; union with him lies as a far distant ideal before the eye of the soul. Yet there is also a certainty that this union will not be possible until all the powers which have come to the initiate from this world are applied by him to liberating and redeeming it. If he resolves to fulfil the demands of this higher being of light, the initiate will be able to contribute to the liberation of the human race. He brings his gifts to the altar of humanity. [...]

28. Humanity Resurrected

Extract from a lecture given in Cologne on 11 April 1909

The final passage in this volume offers an eloquent summation of many of its themes and a panoramic view of humanity's possible future development towards the 'eternal I', to which, if we allow it, a science of the spirit can summon us. The ailing Amfortas in us, both as individuals and as the whole of humanity, can be healed if we open ourselves to the source of healing we already bear within us as potential through Christ's deed.

[...] If, 600 years before our era, entrance into the physical augured suffering for human beings, how does the great truth that life is suffering present itself to the soul after the Mystery of Golgotha? How does it present itself to those who look with understanding at the cross on Golgotha? Is birth, as the Buddha declared, suffering? Those who look with understanding at the cross on Golgotha, and feel united with it, say to themselves: 'Birth, after all, leads us to an earth that is able, from its own elements, to provide a raiment for the Christ. We will gladly tread this earth upon which Christ has walked. Union with Christ kindles in the soul the power to find its way up into the spiritual worlds, brings the realization that birth is not suffering but the gateway through which one must pass to find the Redeemer, who clothed Himself with the very same earthly substances which compose the bodily frame of a human being.'

Is illness suffering? No!—so said those who truly understood the impulse of Golgotha—no, illness is not suffering. Even if people cannot yet understand what the spiritual life streaming in with Christ is in reality, in future they will learn to understand it, and they will know that someone who allows the Christ impulse to permeate him, into whose innermost being the Christ power draws, can overcome all illness through the strong healing forces he unfolds from within himself. For Christ is the great healer of humanity. His power embraces everything that the spiritual can unfold as healing forces, through which illness can be overcome. Illness is not suffering. Illness is an opportunity to overcome limitations and hindrances by unfolding the Christ power within ourselves.

Mankind must arrive at a similar understanding about the infirmities of age. The more the feebleness of our limbs increases, the more we can grow in the spirit, the more we can gain self-mastery through the Christ power indwelling us. Age is not suffering, for with every day that passes we grow into the spiritual world. So too, death is not suffering for it has been conquered in the Resurrection. Death has been conquered through the event of Golgotha.

Can separation from what we love still be suffering? No! Souls permeated with the Christ power know that love can forge links from soul to soul transcending all material obstacles, links in the spiritual that cannot be severed; and there is nothing either in the life between birth and death or between death and rebirth to which we cannot spiritually find the way through the Christ impulse. If we permeate ourselves with the Christ impulse, permanent separation from what we love is inconceivable. The Christ leads us to union with what we love.

Equally, to be united with what we do not love cannot be suffering because the Christ impulse received into our souls teaches us to love all things in their due measure. The Christ

HGRAIL
HGRAYL

impulse shows us the way and, when we find this way, 'to be united with what we do not love' can no longer be suffering; for there is nothing that we do not encompass with love. So too, if Christ is with us, 'not to attain what we yearn for' can no longer be suffering, for human feelings and desires are so purified and sublimated through the Christ impulse that people can yearn only for what is their due. They no longer suffer because of what they are compelled to renounce; for if they must renounce anything, it is for the sake of purification, and the Christ power enables them to feel it as such. Therefore renunciation is no longer suffering. [...]

Now the outer, physical expression for the 'I' is the blood. This is a great mystery; but there have always been people who knew of it and were aware that replicas of the 'I' of Jesus of Nazareth are present in the spiritual world. There have always been people whose task it was, through the centuries since the event of Golgotha, to ensure in secret that humanity gradually matures, so that there may be human beings who are fit to receive the replicas of the 'I' of Jesus Christ of Nazareth, just as there were those who received replicas of His etheric body and astral body. For this purpose it was necessary to discover the secret of how, in the still depths of a profound mystery, this 'I' might be preserved until the appropriate moment in the evolution of the earth and of humanity. With this aim a brotherhood of initiates who preserved the secret was founded: the brotherhood of the Holy Grail. They were the guardians of this secret. This fellowship has always existed. It is said that its originator took the chalice used by Christ Jesus at the Last Supper and caught in it the blood flowing from the wounds of the Redeemer on the cross. He gathered the blood, the expression of the 'I' in this chalice—the Holy Grail. And the chalice with the blood of the Redeemer, with the secret of the replica of the 'I' of Christ Jesus, was preserved in a holy place, guarded by the brotherhood of those whose attainments and initiation fit them to be brothers of the Holy Grail.

Today the time has arrived when these secrets may be made known, when through a spiritual life human hearts can become mature enough to understand this great Mystery. If souls allow spiritual science to kindle understanding of such secrets they become fit to recognize in that holy chalice the mystery of the Christ-'I,' the eternal 'I' which every human 'I' can become. The secret is a reality—only people must allow spiritual science to summon them to understand this, in order that, as they contemplate the Holy Grail, the Christ-'I' may be received into their being. To this end they must understand and accept what has come to pass as fact, as reality.

But when people are better prepared to receive the Christ-I, it will pour in greater and greater fullness into their souls. They will then evolve to the level where Christ Jesus stood, their great exemplar. Then for the first time they will learn to understand the sense in which Christ Jesus is humanity's great exemplar. And having understood this, they will begin to realize in the inmost core of their being that the certainty of life's eternity springs from the corpse hanging on the wood of the cross of Golgotha. Those who are inspired and permeated by the Christ-'I', the Christians of future time, will understand something else as well—something that hitherto has been known only to those who reached enlightenment. They will understand not only the Christ who passed through death but the triumphant Christ of the Apocalypse, resurrected in the spiritual fire, the Christ whose coming has already been predicted. The Easter festival can always be for us a symbol of the risen one, a link reaching from Christ on the cross to the Christ triumphant, risen and glorified, to the one who lifts all human beings with Him to the right hand of the Father.

And so the Easter symbol points us to the vista of the whole future of the earth, to the future of the evolution of humanity, and is for us a guarantee that those who are Christ-inspired will be transformed from Saul-people into Paul-people and will behold a spiritual fire with increasing clarity. It is indeed true that just as the Christ was revealed in advance to Moses and to those who were with him, in the material fire of the thorn bush and of the lightning on Sinai, so He will be revealed to us in a spiritualized fire of the future. He is with us always, until the end of the world, and He will appear in the spiritual fire to those who have allowed their eyes to be enlightened through the event of Golgotha. Human beings will behold Him in the spiritual fire. They beheld Him, to begin with, in a different form; they will behold Him for the first time in His true form, in a spiritual fire.

But because the Christ penetrated so deeply into earth-existence—right into the physical bony structure—the power which built His sheaths out of the elements of the earth so purified and hallowed this physical substance that it can never become what in their sorrow the eastern sages feared. They believed that the enlightened one of the future, the Maitreya Buddha, would not find on earth human beings capable of understanding him because they had sunk so deeply into matter. Christ was led to Golgotha that He might raise matter again to spiritual heights, so that the fire might not be extinguished in matter, but be spiritualized. Primal wisdom will again be intelligible to human beings when they themselves are spiritualized—the primal wisdom which, in the spiritual world, was the source of their being. And so the Maitreya Buddha will find understanding on the earth—which would not otherwise have been possible—when human beings have attained deeper insight. We understand far better what we learnt in our youth when the trials of life have matured us, and we can look back upon it all at a later time. Humanity will again come to understand the primal wisdom by looking back upon it in the Christ light streaming from the event of Golgotha.

Notes and references

1. I have used Wolfram's designation, rather than Wagner's 'Parsifal' or Chrétien de Troyes's 'Perceval'. Clearly these names and their derivations are all closely related.
2. These names refer to successive stages of planetary evolution in Steiner's cosmology, from which our present earth developed.
3. In Steiner's view we possess, apart from our mineralized physical body, an etheric or life body which we share with the plant kingdom, and an astral or soul body which we have in common with animals. The etheric body is chiefly associated with rhythms, circulation and habitual ways of doing things, while the astral body is the seat of passions, emotions and soul. The fourth, and eternal aspect of our being is the 'I' or ego which continues to exist after death and subsequently seeks reincarnation in a new body. Through this most spiritual aspect we can gradually transform the 'lower' bodies (see also note 31).
4. This is a reference to the Archangel Michael who now, once again, presides over human evolution in our era and who is closely connected with encouraging the overcoming of barriers of nation and race to form a global human community. At the same time he is a being for whom our free actions are essential, and who waits for us to develop our own spiritual impetus.
5. 'Viaticum' literally means 'provision for the journey'. Its use in Christian ritual is explained as follows: 'The celebration of the Eucharist as viaticum, food for the passage through death to eternal life, is the sacrament proper to the dying Christian. It is the completion and crown of the Christian life on this earth, signifying that the Christian follows the Lord to eternal glory and the banquet of the heavenly kingdom.' (http://www.deacons.net/Articles/Viaticum.htm)

6. Translation by M. Cotterell, revised by M. Barton.
7. One might presumably see the waxing and waning moon here, in connection with the viaticum, as symbolic of a complementary decrease and increase of physical or spiritual life; and this in turn reminds one of the St John the Baptist's utterance: 'I must decrease and He must increase.'
8. See note 2.
9. See note 2. Vulcan is the last planetary embodiment, where human evolution will reach its provisional culmination and fulfilment.
10. R.M. Rilke: *Letters to a Young Poet*, Vintage 1986.
11. Parzival saw knights riding in the forest, and therefore discovered such beings existed.
12. Chrétien de Troyes (c.1143–c.1190). French poet living at the courts of Champagne and Flanders. He established epic poetry at the courts and was its most important practitioner. His epics include those of Lancelot and Perceval.
13. *Parzival* by Wolfram von Eschenbach was composed around 1200–1210 and first printed in 1477. It was then forgotten for many years and only rediscovered around 1750. The first critical edition was published by Lachmann in 1833 and followed by numerous others. English translations: J.L. Weston, *A Knightly Epic*, in verse, 2 vols, London 1894; Mustard and Passage, *Parzival*, Vintage Books, New York 1961; A.T. Hatto, *Parzival*, Penguin Classics 1980.
14. This is a story also found in Schiller's poem 'The veiled image at Sais' (a place in Egypt).
15. Luke 22:19.
16. Lucifer and Ahriman are the two polar forces of evil in Steiner's cosmology. Lucifer tempts us away from the earth while Ahriman fetters us to it. Christ is the balancing mediator between these two.
17. According to Steiner, Ancient Lemuria was a continent between the present continents of Asia, Africa, and Australia,

and was inhabited by a very different humanity. It preceded the Atlantean age, and during this early period of earth evolution the moon separated from the earth.

18. In the Bible, in contrast, these words are rendered as: 'My God, My God, Why hast thou forsaken me?' See Judith von Halle, *And If He Has Not Been Raised*... Temple Lodge 2007, for more on this apparent discrepancy.
19. *Der arme Heinrich* by Hartmann von Aue.
20. Minnesänger were troubadours who sang of spiritualized or ideal love.
21. Kundry is an ambiguous figure. In other passages and versions of the saga, she also acts as a force for good and as an emissary of the Grail. She often seems to act in a challenging role, to test other characters' real accomplishments, and thus can be a spur to their higher development.
22. Wisdom, beauty, strength. See passages below for further elaboration.
23. Lord Lytton: *The Coming Race*, George Routledge and Sons, London 1870. At Steiner's instigation, Günther Wachsmuth translated the novel into German under the title *Vril oder eine Menscheit der Zukunft*. In an answer to a question to Rudolf Steiner at the end of a lecture on 13 October 1906, he said the following about the meaning of *Vril*:

    Everything which was previously present in the world will return again. The Vril force or power underlies something special. At present man can really only make use of the forces of the mineral world. Gravity is a mineral power, electricity also. The building of railways is due to coal. What human beings cannot yet do, however, is use the power of plants. The force which causes blades of corn to spring up in a cornfield is a still latent power which human beings will press into their service, just as they have coal. That is Vril. It is the same power fakirs still use, drawing on an ancestral atavism.

24. From the Middle Ages onwards.
25. According to Steiner, the Akashic Record retains a supersensible memory of everything human beings have ever thought, felt or done.
26. As human beings evolved they passed through various 'soul' stages.
27. Earlier in this lecture Steiner says: 'These external pictures point to the endeavours of human souls in refining and purifying forces of the astral body which presented themselves to the seer as images of monsters, giants and the like.'
28. A quote from Schiller in his play 'Homage to the Arts'.
29. See passage on page 159.
30. That is, increasingly degenerate: a physical body that was less and less permeable for spirit.
31. The 'life spirit' is a transformation of the human etheric body that occurs on the path of higher development. The transformed astral body is called the 'spirit self', and the transformed ego the 'spirit man'.
32. See *Knowledge of the Higher Worlds*.

List of sources

Numbers relate to section numbers in this volume

1. Hamburg, 18 May 1908, in: *The Gospel of St John*, GA 103, Anthroposophic Press 1984
2. Kassel, 24 June 1909, in: *The Gospel of St John in its Relation to the Other Three Gospels*, GA 112, Anthroposophic Press 1982
3. (i) Torquay, 21 August 1924, in: *Karmic Relationships, vol. VIII*, GA 240, Rudolf Steiner Press 1975
   (ii) Torquay, 27 August 1924, in: *Karmic Relationships, vol. VIII*, GA 240, Rudolf Steiner Press 1975
4. Chapter 6 in *Occult Science*, GA 13 ('Present and Future Evolution of the World and Mankind'), Rudolf Steiner Press 1979
5. Leipzig, 1 January 1914, in: *Christ and the Spiritual World. The Search for the Holy Grail*, GA 149, Rudolf Steiner Press 1983
6. Leipzig, 2 January 1914, in: *Christ and the Spiritual World. The Search for the Holy Grail*, GA 149, Rudolf Steiner Press 1983
7. Berlin, 6 January 1914, in: *The Fifth Gospel*, GA 148, Rudolf Steiner Press 1995
8. Dornach, 16 April 1921, in: *Materialism and the Task of Anthroposophy*, GA 204, Anthroposophic Press / Rudolf Steiner Press 1987
9. Dornach, 17 April 1921, in: *Materialism and the Task of Anthroposophy*, GA 204, Anthroposophic Press / Rudolf Steiner Press 1987
10. Berlin, 1 April 1907, in: *The Christian Mystery* (from GA 96), Anthroposophic Press 1998
11. Berlin, 19 May 1905, in: *Richard Wagner in the Light of*

Anthroposophy (from GA 92), typescript NSL 175–8, Rudolf Steiner House library, London

12. Nuremberg, 2 December 1907, in: *Anthroposophy* (from GA 92), Midsummer 1930, vol. 5, no. 2
13. Stuttgart, 16 September 1907, in: *Occult Signs and Symbols*, GA 101, Anthroposophic Press 1972
14. Berlin, 6 January 1906, in: *The Temple Legend*, GA 93, Rudolf Steiner Press 1985
15. Berlin, 2 July 1913, in: *Mysteries of the East and of Christianity*, GA 144, Rudolf Steiner Press 1972
16. Dornach, 11 March 1923, in: *The Driving Force of Spiritual Powers in World History*, GA 222, Steiner Book Centre 1972
17. The Hague, 26 March 1913, in: *The Effects of Esoteric Development*, GA 145, Anthroposophic Press 1997
18. Dornach, 22 October 1922, in: *Spiritual Relations in the Human Organism*, GA 218, Mercury Press 1984
19. Prague, 28 March 1911, in: *An Occult Physiology*, GA 128, Rudolf Steiner Press 2005
20. (i) Dornach, 9 November 1923, in: *Harmony of the Creative Word*, GA 240, Rudolf Steiner Press 2001
    (ii) Dornach, 10 November 1923, in: *Harmony of the Creative Word*, GA 240, Rudolf Steiner Press 2001
21. Dornach, 16 May 1920, in: *Mystery of the Universe*, GA 201, Rudolf Steiner Press 2001
22. The Hague, 25 March 1913, in: *The Effects of Spiritual Development*, GA 145, Anthroposophic Press 1997
23. Basel, 1 October 1911, in *Esoteric Christianity*, GA 130, Rudolf Steiner Press 2000
24. Munich, 6 June 1907, in: *Rosicrucian Wisdom (Theosophy of the Rosicrucian)*, GA 99, Rudolf Steiner Press 2000
25. Munich, 6 June 1907, in: *Guidance in Esoteric Training*, GA 245, Rudolf Steiner Press 1998
26. Berlin, 6 May 1909, in: *Anthroposophical Quarterly* (from GA 57), spring 1964